What people are saying about . .

Zachar...

"*Zachary's Choice* is soul-bearing and gives voice to the silent agony of all suicide survivors. I felt like I was there and heard the deep crying sound of pain that most people will never hear. This is a story of strength and hope that will touch everyone who carries our cross."

John Shockley, lost fifteen-year-old son, Johnny, in 2009

"Suzy's ability to articulate the darkness of grief, the stigma of suicide, and the comfort of Christ is a gift to those living the aftermath of such tragedy. This book grants the bereaved permission to experience the weight of grief without judgment, yet points them to the relentless love of the Holy Comforter. *Zachary's Choice* is a sanctuary for those who know the trauma of suicide and child death and an invaluable resource for those who desire to minister to suicide survivors."

Regina Cyzick Harlow, bereaved mom,
pastor, grief companion, and founder
of The Sadie Rose Foundation

"After losing my forty-five-year-old brother to suicide, I felt totally lost and alone. The darkness was almost too much to bear. This sincere book shows that God loves me and holds me in the palm of His hand. It will help anyone dealing with the horror and shame of suicide."

Tammy S. Whitmer, lost brother, Mike, in 2010

"'Things like this don't happen to Christian, homeschooling families, do they?' This quote from *Zachary's Choice* sums up this deeply expressive memoir about a teen's suicide that appears to have come from nowhere. Instead of a warning to parents, this book, written by a dedicated mother and foster mother, serves as a comfort to survivors.

This memoir is evidence of the limited power we have over others and addresses the guilt and public shame often associated with a suicide death. *Zachary's Choice* would be a great resource for people who want to help a survivor but have no experience with suicide."

Ginny Sparrow, editor, American
Association of Suicidology

"As Suzy described her feelings throughout her journey, they were reminiscent of my own. This honest book will be a blessing to so many women."

Lori Wyatt, lost sixteen-year-old
son, Nicholas, in 1995

"In her memoir, *Zachary's Choice*, Suzy LaBonte candidly explores the full spectrum of emotions associated with loss by suicide. She confronts the nagging 'whys,' the guilt and shame, and the difficult process of moving on. With humility, honesty, and grace, Suzy inspires hope that true joy is possible even after confronting one of life's most tragic losses—the death of a child by suicide."

Lisa Ellison, Ed.S, NCC, Resident in Counseling,
lost twenty-year-old brother, Joe, in 1997

"Finally, an unguarded book that tells the personal and intimate side of what suicide does to the ones left behind. *Zachary's Choice* has shown me that I'm not alone in this journey and that all of my intense and unpredictable emotions are acceptable. Anyone who has lost a loved one to suicide should read this book."

Stephanie L. Darne, lost husband, Sgt.
Matthew C. Darne USMC, in 2013

ZACHARY'S CHOICE

SURVIVING MY CHILD'S SUICIDE

SUZY LABONTE

ZACHARY'S CHOICE

SURVIVING MY CHILD'S SUICIDE

David C Cook®
transforming lives together

ZACHARY'S CHOICE
Published by David C Cook
4050 Lee Vance View
Colorado Springs, CO 80918 U.S.A.

David C Cook Distribution Canada
55 Woodslee Avenue, Paris, Ontario, Canada N3L 3E5

David C Cook U.K., Kingsway Communications
Eastbourne, East Sussex BN23 6NT, England

The graphic circle C logo is a registered trademark of David C Cook.

The website addresses recommended throughout this book are offered as a
resource to you. These websites are not intended in any way to be or imply an
endorsement on the part of David C Cook, nor do we vouch for their content.

All Scripture quotations are taken from the Holy Bible, New International
Version®, NIV®. Copyright © 1973, 1984 by Biblica, Inc.™ Used by permission
of Zondervan. All rights reserved worldwide. www.zondervan.com.

ISBN 978-0-7814-1317-6
eISBN 978-0-7814-1294-0

© 2014 Suzy LaBonte

The Team: Renada Thompson, Susan Murdock, Karen Athen
Cover Design: Nick Lee
Cover Photo: Shutterstock
Photo of Zachary by Picture Me.

Printed in the United States of America
First Edition 2014

1 2 3 4 5 6 7 8 9 10

100114

CONTENTS

*Dedicated to all of the children who wanted to live
but found it too painful to do so,
and to each of their loved ones who
are surviving such a thing.*

ZACHARY LEE LABONTE
November 7, 1992 - March 6, 2009

A NOTE TO
THE READER

On March 6, 2009, my beautiful and talented sixteen-year-old son, Zachary, took his own life without prior threat or forewarning. The days and months that followed were unbearably confusing, achingly sad, and riddled with relentless guilt. I grieved hard and long, trying to make sense of both Zachary's suicide and the significant effect his agonizing death was beginning to have on every area of my life.

My life changed forever on a single Friday afternoon, yet the God I had on that tragic day is the same faithful and good Father I knew the day before. He gave grace to my confusion with a faithful love that patiently sustained my life. As the truest of fathers, He stepped into my darkness and grieved alongside me on the blackest of nights. Slowly, with God's tender mercies and many supportive loved ones, I began to heal and reclaim my life.

This is not a story I wanted to tell, nor a journey I wanted to document. It is instead the result of a deeply personal journal that provided a safe place for the many different, painful emotions to exist during the heartbreaking months following my son's death. More than just a book about unexpected suicide, this is a story about God's sustaining power amid a horrific and confusing family tragedy.

It is likely that you have picked up this book because your life has been touched by the confusion and horror of a loved one's suicide, and I am truly sorry that you find yourself reading its pages. It is my hope that this story will help you in some small way to make sense of this journey of survival and give you comfort, knowing you are not alone. Healing after the devastation of a loved one's suicide is truly possible, and each of us can find hope to not only survive, but to one day fully thrive.

My prayer for sharing Zachary's story is to offer a measure of healing and encouragement to those suffering from a suicide loss. If the ministry of this book offers any renewal of hope and life, then beauty will have been created from the ashes. I think Zachary, if he could look down from heaven, would be pleased.

You may contact the author at zacharyschoice@juno.com or visit zachary-labonte.memory-of.com to view photos and more memories of Zachary.

ACKNOWLEDGMENTS

I would like to say thank you to all of the many friends, neighbors, family members, and dear ones at our church who walked with our family through this dark valley. At times, you spoke wisdom and blessed us with your words. At other times, you said very little and comforted us with your presence. You watched us trudge and stumble and have been a host of earthly angels, caring for us and our children in many creative ways, especially in the days immediately following Zachary's death. We are grateful that we did not have to carry the burden of his death alone.

I have been honored to meet and become familiar with many who have lost a loved one to suicide, both in my community and beyond. Thank you for letting me share in your sorrow as you have in mine, for hearing your stories continues to give me strength to acknowledge and process my own. Thank you for supporting this book project and for encouraging me to use Zachary's story to minister to others.

Thank you to our extended family—great-grandparents, grandparents, aunts, uncles, sisters, brothers, and cousins—for loving, nurturing, encouraging, and teaching Zachary throughout the years. Each of you who rejoiced with us at his birth and enjoyed his life sorrowed deeply with us at his death. You blessed Zachary with many faithful prayers, silly birthday cards, and thoughtful Christmas gifts. You read him stories, taught him about life, and applauded his every accomplishment. You cultivated deeply and lovingly invested in his character and contributed richly to the person he became. Thank you for your living examples of Christianity.

I thank and honor our birth children and fellow survivors— Nicholas, Jesse, Emily, and Lydia. To have given birth to, nurtured, and raised each of you continues to be the deepest honor of my life. My existence revolves around you, driven by a love that is both immense and eternal, and I am so proud of all that you are becoming. Thank you for loving me despite my imperfections. As your parent, I thought myself to be the one doing the teaching, yet it is your resilience and optimistic courage that has inspired me. I am sorry that you had to endure such pain at your tender ages, and it is my continual prayer that the loss of your brother will shape you into even stronger and more compassionate people. I miss him too. Thank you for being such great siblings to Zachary; he was blessed to have you.

To the many wonderful children who joined our family through foster care adoption, I love you. Zachary would have adored each of you and carried you proudly on his shoulders. I am sorry that you never really knew your big brother. We will do our best to teach you who he was.

To Allen, my trustworthy best friend who has kept and honored his promise to love me "for better or for worse," thank you for being there above and beyond the call of duty. It is your love that pulled me through the darkest moments, for your arms have never failed to hold me together when I totally fall apart. You are one of the wisest people I know, and I thank you for authentically living the gospel in your confident, calm way. You are a wonderful father to our children, and I dream of that moment when you are happily reunited with Zachary in heaven.

And above all else, I thank God for choosing Allen and me to be Zachary's parents, for entrusting his little life into our care, and for allowing us to love and enjoy this wonderful and creative person for sixteen years. I cling to each memory with gratefulness, for surely our lives were enriched by such a child.

Lastly, to Zachary, thank you for letting me share your story, for it continues to have a glorious unfolding of unexpected and amazing twists. Satan meant your death for destruction, but many are now receiving encouragement and comfort from their own pain because of the healing work God has created from your death. You are loved beyond words and missed beyond measure. I can't wait to see you again.

1

BLINDSIDED BY SUICIDE

My soul finds rest in God alone;
my salvation comes from him.
He alone is my rock and my salvation;
he is my fortress, I will never be shaken.

Psalm 62:1–3

It was a beautiful day to be alive.

The morning of March 6, 2009, felt like the first day of spring as I stood peacefully on the front porch of our country home admiring the brightness of the dewy grass and breathing in the clean air around me. Scattered throughout the yard in an eagerness to make their appearance after many weeks of winter's harsh cold, the first early clumps of daffodils boasted large, hopeful buds. As I appreciated the beauty of the mountains in the distance, it felt delicious to inhale dawn's sweetness and feel the sun's warmth soak deep into my pale arms. The enthusiastic morning songbirds further lightened my mood.

I was a homeschooling mother of five birth children ages ten through eighteen and a foster parent to two young preschoolers. On this beautiful morning, Allen and our oldest son had left for work. As I watched the children run in the grass like playful lambs too long cooped up, I regretted that on this beautiful day I had afternoon appointments to keep and errands to run.

Zachary, sixteen, wanted to stay home. I thought nothing unusual of his choice and confidently decided to leave two children home with him. He was a bright and sensitive boy. Gifted in art and known for being silly and fun loving, he was a good student, a hard worker, and a responsible son. He had never abused my trust in any way, and I totally valued his judgment. After a quick lunch and a few casual good-byes, the remaining three children and I climbed into the van and were soon on our way.

I ran my errands, bought some groceries, picked up several pizzas for dinner, and headed home. Off work a little early, my husband, Allen, pulled in behind us around 4:30 and helped the children lug the plastic bags of groceries through the front door while I stashed the cold foods in the fridge. The steaming pizzas were set on the table as the children kicked off their shoes and scattered throughout the house in great preparation to eat. With excited clamoring, family members of all sizes headed to the kitchen table, grabbing plates and claiming sodas on the way.

But no one knew where Zachary was. He wasn't in his room or in the bathroom. Hadn't he heard the van on the gravel driveway? Hadn't he heard us bursting through the front door or heard us shouting his name as we raced through the house?

It didn't feel right to eat without Zachary. I personally rechecked every room of the house to conclude that he wasn't anywhere in it.

Concern heightened, but I assumed he probably just went outside to do his chores, get the mail, or care for the many golden retrievers we raised.

One child ran to check the barn and another hurried to look in the workshop. No one could find Zachary. This was out of the norm. The Friday afternoon party mood was quickly fading as the faces sobered around the cooling pizza, now losing its appetizing appeal. The panic was quickly rising in my throat.

I could not find my son.

We continued looking around the property, trying to think logically of where he might have gone. Someone offered to check the woods behind our house. Urgency was deepening like the long afternoon shadows. Anxiety and fear were heightening as the March sunshine was quickly turning into afternoon chill.

I needed to find my son.

Suddenly, one of the teenage boys came stumbling out of the woods with a breathless, gasping report. Wearing a horrific and fearful expression, he said that Zachary was lying on the ground bleeding.

Receiving this child's terrifying account and watching him stand before me in fear trying to catch his breath, I had a strange feeling in the pit of my stomach that one of my children had set his eyes on something that no child should ever see. I had a strange feeling in that moment that this boy was much too innocent and naïve, far too young and childlike, to have come upon his brother lying in the woods as he did. I wished I had refused his quick offer to search, wished I had done everything in my power to keep him close to me, wished I had sent him back inside the house to reheat the pizza or serve some to the younger children.

But what was done, was done.

My husband quickly followed my son's wild gesturing toward the woods while my shaking legs took me to a phone and I called 911. I knew so little, had such few facts to report, and could only request help. "My son is bleeding. In the woods. Please hurry!" I said, giving my address. "No, I don't know what is wrong. I don't know what has happened."

I got off the phone and ran outside, yelling orders over my shoulder for the children to stay in the house. By this time, Allen had returned from the woods, winded and shocked. Reading his facial features, I tried to interpret expressions I did not recognize. A queer chill rushed down my spine. I knew in one instant that something was terribly wrong. I knew intuitively in one moment that my life was changing forever.

Allen pulled off his hat and threw it to the ground in anger and frustration. "I think he is dead," he choked, trying to catch his breath. Collapsing on the bench near our front door, he threw his hands up over his face in disbelief and shock. "I think he killed himself."

Those moments are forever imprinted in my memory, branding themselves as a hot iron identifies livestock. I will never forget the way Allen spoke those piercing words to me or uncharacteristically hurled his hat to the ground. I will never forget the weight of that horrible message crushing my chest and forcing the breath out of my lungs. In one moment, my life veered chaotically off a well-constructed course.

"What?" I said, my heart racing with terror and confusion. "What?"

"He had a gun. I think he killed himself."

Although received as a stinging slap, the repeated statement did not in any way compute. My hand flew to cover my gaping mouth. I was utterly and completely confused.

"Take me," I said, hoping that maybe there had just been some misunderstanding amid the confusion. Perhaps if everyone just calmed down a bit, we would all find out that nothing serious had occurred after all. I might even be able to fix this.

"Take me to him," I demanded, hoping desperately that this was all just a big mistake, an absurd misunderstanding.

Sick with fear and disbelief, I followed Allen into the woods and up the hill. With heart pounding and legs trembling, I felt my life physically unraveling like a thick woolen sweater and was certain I was leaving a trail of yarn behind myself. Shaking and trembling, we quickly ran a few hundred yards.

Then we stopped and my nightmare continued.

From fifty feet away, I saw my precious child for the very last time. I wanted to get closer, but Allen held me back. I argued and wrestled to be free. Allen insisted. Something finally told me he knew better, and I submitted to his protection. Leaning against a tree, I struggled to catch my breath and calm my beating heart. Wave after wave of terror swept over me.

How could this be? What on earth had happened? We yelled the questions at each other, knowing neither of us had the answers. My mind responded like a computer screen: Does not compute! Does not compute!

We had no time to stand there dazed. Fully understanding that there was a waiting and worrying band of children to report to, we turned, shocked, with hearts pounding, and rallied together for the inevitable return back to the house.

How would we tell the children? Did Zachary really kill himself? Did we even know that for sure? What should we say? Would it be okay to stall for time and just break the news that he was dead?

Agreeing that this gentle plan would be best, we quickly left that place of defeat feeling as if we had just seen something we weren't supposed to have witnessed. We stumbled back over the tree roots, ignoring the thorny brambles tearing at our arms, and wildly rushed toward the house with the horrible news.

Inside the kitchen, we stepped back into the roles we knew so well. With love and as much gentleness as possible—while strangely aware that these moments would be permanently seared into our children's tender minds—we guarded our words to ensure a gentle delivery and told the anxious children that their brother was dead.

The crying began. The children fell apart, their hearts crumbling into fragments. I witnessed before me a physical shattering of innocence and trust and instinctively knew their souls were changing before my eyes. As their faces contorted into emotions I had never before witnessed, I hated that these, who I had spent my entire life protecting, had now been exposed to such pain. The sorrowful wailing was unlike anything I had ever heard, and I could do nothing to either silence or ease it.

How could Zachary have done this to his siblings? His two teenage brothers, one younger and one older, had experienced all of childhood with him in an elite band of brotherhood. How could he have done this to his two little sisters who looked up to him, adored him, and secretly enjoyed his constant teasing? What about the preschoolers that he enjoyed carrying around? How on earth would we explain this death to each innocent mind?

How could Zachary have done this to us, his parents? Were we not enough for him? Did we not make his life worth living? Had he considered how we would feel to find him dead? Did the fact that he had a loving family totally elude him?

There was no time to think.

The frenzy arrived shortly in the form of rescue workers and police officers. Their arrival made me feel safe. These skilled and trained professionals were in control now. Perhaps these uniformed experts could sort out this craziness and undo whatever madness had happened in the woods.

Proficiently they went to the place where they were directed and returned promptly to verify what we already knew. Zachary was dead. It appeared he had shot himself. With a brief and curt, "I'm sorry, ma'am," the rescue workers left just as quickly as they had arrived. How I wished they would have stayed and done something. How I wished they had been needed in some kind of search and rescue and that their hands could have worked a miracle to restore life.

The police, however, lingered dutifully to begin their investigation. Swarming our house and speaking garbled somber messages into their radios, the officers took photos of the incident site and walked our property. I felt like my beloved country home had become more of a crime scene than the safe haven I so enjoyed. The necessary questioning felt invasive, as if I were party to a crime or responsible for a scandal. Guilt began to seep steadily into my heart.

The children, ever watchful, were gathering bits and pieces of the unfolding drama. Most were hearing the word *suicide* for the first time and demanding an explanation for that term. Some stood quietly shocked and stunned while several sat stricken with panic and fear. Others were hanging on me, crying hysterically with anguished and disbelieving cries. "Why did he do that? Why did he hurt himself?"

Trying to manage the utter chaos that swirled around me and somehow emitting a confidence I did not feel, to the best of my limited ability, I answered the many confusing questions being hurled at me from both family and professionals. Focused on calming the children, I offered comfort where it was needed, and could only answer their confusion with my own, "I do not know ... I do not know."

One serious fresh-faced officer came into the house with eyes too young for an issue so grave. He gently asked if there was a note or any talk of suicide and wanted to see Zachary's room. His questioning continued as his pen scrawled facts on the clipboard. Names? Ages? Birthdates? Social Security numbers? His young face was hidden under his cap's brim, and he glanced up at me only now and then to nod. I wondered if keeping his eyes on his paperwork was easier than looking into mine.

As the madness heightened, I maintained a vigilant watch over what was left of my traumatized, fractured family. I monitored Allen's every move, waiting for his wisdom to clarify this disorder. Surely, I was in a bad dream. Surely, I would wake up any minute. Zachary can't be dead—he just can't be.

Allen called our pastors and one quickly came to the house with his wife, shocked and full of concern. These dear ones stood quietly beside us as the questioning continued. Another pastor arrived, took one look at us, and immediately began to cry. These men both knew my son well and had taught Zachary's youth classes at church. As shocked as I was about his death, there was no need for words—their compassionate embraces were enough.

Evidence revealed that Zachary had taken a spare set of keys, unlocked the workshop, and found a pair of bolt cutters to cut the lock on an ammunition box. Getting what he needed, he relocked the shop and returned the keys to their proper drawer. When we questioned the younger siblings who had been home at the time, we found that during this entire process, Zachary had apparently checked several times to make sure his younger siblings were occupied in the living room watching TV.

I was astounded that in his final moments, Zachary had been organized and rational. I was amazed that he had been careful to make sure no one saw him gathering the things he needed to end his life. I believe with certainty that Zachary's secretive planning was in part to shield the younger children. He was still being a thoughtful, considerate person, a protective big brother, even at his death.

Finally, sure that he could carry out his task in secret, Zachary had exited a back door of the house and slipped into our woods to complete his plan. I will forever be grateful to him for the decision to quietly take his death outside. Oddly enough, in those last moments of his life, it was a final gift to our family.

The authorities had summoned the funeral home attendants who quietly arrived, shook our hands respectfully, and backed their vehicle to the edge of the woods. They walked the very same path that Zachary took and went together with the police and one pastor to remove Zachary's body from the woods.

I stood in the grass and watched from a distance with our oldest son who had just raced home from work to be greeted by this shocking commotion of his brother's death. March's springtime weather of the morning had been a tease, and the air now had a chilly nip. I folded my arms across my chest to warm myself as I waited for the men to return, bringing the truth with them. I couldn't help but notice that the evening sky was a deep and beautiful shade of blue.

Finally, the men walked back out of the woods in a kind of funeral procession, slowly carrying our son. I thought of Zachary's beautiful, strong, vibrant, healthy body and could not imagine it now limp, still, cold, and broken with defeat in both body and spirit.

Barely able to see in the rapidly deepening darkness, I stood from afar and watched them gently load Zachary's precious body into their vehicle. Feeling the chill of evening seep into my heart, I could not take my eyes off the black SUV as it proceeded to the driveway.

The funeral director then came into the house and, in hushed tones, told us what he expected would happen in the next few days. Zachary's body would need to be sent for an autopsy in another city to confirm that his death was a suicide. When it was returned to the funeral home, he and our pastors would help us determine when a memorial service and burial would be planned. With a thin smile, the funeral director handed us a business card and some papers with phone numbers. And did we have any questions?

"None," I said solemnly, while at the same time mindful of many escalating in my mind. "None that you would probably be able to answer."

This kind man, who was obviously so accustomed to death, gave me a sad nod and started to leave. As he turned and put his hand on the doorknob to quietly open it, I saw thick drying blood on the back of his hand. I couldn't take my eyes off it. It was the last little piece of Zachary I ever saw.

From the initial 911 call at five o'clock until the funeral director left with my son's body, it had taken only three hours for the authorities to come, investigate, verify, give their professional condolences, and leave. Three hours prior, I had been pulling into the driveway preparing to happily eat hot pizza with my family. Three hours prior, I hadn't a single care in the world, and as far as I knew, my family was merely hungry and very much intact. My biggest concern had been getting the melting ice cream into the freezer. I had never tasted such sorrow nor such terror. Now three hours seemed a lifetime ago. I knew I would never be going back to my prior life.

Eight o'clock and for the first time, I noticed the full shopping bags still sprawled all over the kitchen floor. Groceries seemed inconsequential and totally unnecessary in light of what had happened. I scooted one bag under the kitchen table with my foot and looked at the soup can that came rolling out. It was mockery, for in my child's darkest hour, I had been unavailable. Zachary had been despairing while I happily drove through town. My own child had killed himself while I was pondering which breakfast cereal to buy. I had been caught off guard. I was a fool to have ever been so happy. I vowed never to be happy again.

Later that evening after everyone had gone and the preschoolers were taken to bed, our family sat in the darkness of our living room with only one little light on. It was comforting to be together. We sat under blankets, tired and completely overwhelmed, staring straight ahead. No one spoke. We had all asked our questions and received no answers. It was futile to ask again.

Allen and I were used to having all our children home at the end of the day, and the void from Zachary's absence was huge. We did not know how to be apart. It hurt in such a physical way to know he was somewhere, right at that moment, lying in the back of a strange vehicle with a strange driver, going farther and farther away from us, away from his family, away from his life.

No one had the chance to say good-bye.

I stared at the clock and watched the minutes pass, thinking how time was taking my child into his eternity while I was left in the present, in a chilly, dark living room without him. I imagined the angels carrying Zachary, comforting and welcoming him, and then finally escorting him into the loving arms of his Father, Jesus Christ.

Outside the windows, the sky grew drearier and blacker. The structures in my yard—the swing set, the picnic table, and the familiar tall trees that were just preparing to bud—were barely recognizable, for they had all but disappeared into the eerie shadows as if I never knew them.

I closed my eyes in utter devastation. My son was dead. Little did I know that, just as everything familiar was slipping away into the blackness outside my window, my own personal darkness was settling in with resolve, settling in for the long haul.

Night had arrived.

Dear God,

I have spent my entire life devoted to You and have tried to live according to Your principles. You are my Father and I, Your beloved child. Tenderly Your eyes are on me now. Please do not leave or forsake me. Oh, God, I need You now.

2

TELLING OUR LOVED ONES

The Lord is close to the brokenhearted
and saves those who are crushed in spirit.

Psalm 34:18

Later that night, Allen and I took turns dialing the numbers of our relatives and friends. Wincing, and without any luxury of careful timing, we spoke the difficult words, "Zachary is dead. He shot himself." We were unable to cushion the blow and could only speak the news in a blunt and direct manner.

"Yes, suicide. Yes, we are sure. No, we do not know why. No, it was not an accident." Each word was spoken with a cringe. The facts were delivered with confused horror and received in the same way.

"Zachary? Not Zachary! How did it happen? Where? What went wrong? Was there a note? Are you sure it wasn't just a hunting accident?" Questions tumbled into our ears, interrupting the answers we were trying to verbalize.

I spoke with increasing weariness and shame, feeling my own failure and inadequacy as a parent mounting. I soon hated each new phone number, hated every digit, and found myself punching the numbers with rising irritation. Pain pierced through me to utter those words, "Zachary killed himself," for they were words more horrible aloud than they ever would be unspoken.

Every call meant that someone who loved Zachary would be devastated and confused by this crisis. Each call meant one more person would hear that my seemingly happy son had chosen to end his life in a violent way, and like myself, they would be totally unable to comprehend why.

It hurt to imagine that every time we hung up the phone, the one receiving the news of Zachary's death was now forced to share this shocking information with the members of their own household, many of which were children. I ached for our friends, neighbors, and loved ones and sorrowed at the thought of them now sitting shocked in their own quiet living rooms. I hated that I had brought such terror into their homes, for there would be many restless beds tonight.

The phone calls went long into the night as the ripples of Zachary's death reached the hearts and minds of many who loved our family. Grateful for their kind compassion, I watched helplessly as the effect of this tragedy traveled outward like a flat rock forcefully thrown into a lake, breaking the smooth, calm waters of the lives we all had once known.

Finally, there was little else to do. March 6 was almost over. With the last of the children off to bed, Allen and I went to our room but not to sleep. We were overwhelmed with shock and horror. Our child was gone. Gone. Our beautiful life had taken a horrible detour, and this new foreign road felt so off course. How in a million years could such a violent and tragic act have happened to us? We were by no means perfect, but things like this do not happen to Christian homeschooling families, do they?

The world had caved in, and I was suffocating under the weight of its walls crushing my lungs. The pain was excruciating. Shock came from deep inside the pit of my gut, rising out of my throat like vomit. It made me shiver with horror. I felt sick. How could someone without the strength and will to live have such determination and resolve to take his own life? I felt like lying down in agony and bleeding to death.

What was so dreadful that my child had chosen to kill himself? Didn't he know how much we loved, treasured, and appreciated him? What was he thinking? What on earth was he thinking?

How could Zachary have walked out into the woods to shoot himself? How could he have thought a hunting rifle was a good solution to whatever problem he had? This option totally eliminated all others. Why didn't he come to us for help? The magnitude of this total rejection seared my heart, branding me a failure.

Where did we go wrong? I made a list. Had I not balanced my own interests with his needs? Did he not receive enough attention, enough recognition? What made him think his life was already over? Had we contributed to his hopelessness, driven him to his death? The person with the answers could not hear my questions. None of them made sense. All I could do was be sorry we had failed him.

Meticulously I reexamined the last few days. My mind ran backward on the squares of the kitchen calendar. What happened yesterday? Last week? Last month? I looked for clues as I studied the last conversations, the last experiences, and the last hours of Zachary's life.

If only I could go back in time to the morning of his death, alter my trivial plans, change the course of events, and reverse the tragic outcome of Zachary's decision. I wanted to be given five more minutes—just five more minutes to look deeply into his young, green eyes and say three things: "I love you," "I'm so sorry that you hurt," and "What can I do for you?" But I couldn't go back. I could never go back. There was no rewind button, no do-over, and no fairy-tale magic to sprinkle on this cruel curse.

The taunting "if only" ghosts moved into my heart and settled down for their long, harassing stay. If only I had remained home and made sure this never happened. If only I had been more attentive, more affirming. If only I had been more watchful, more observant. If only I had seen some warning signs or noticed his emotional distress.

Self-pity and the unfairness of it all flooded me. Tossing and turning in my bed, all I could do was cry. My beautiful boy ... my beautiful, beautiful boy. He had wasted his precious life with a senseless and irrational act.

What are we going to do? Whatever are we going to do now?

Like mechanical gears slowing down with a descending whine, I could sense every system in my life systematically shutting down. Every bustle and whir from each piece of well-oiled machinery was steadily coming to an eerie halt. Lying motionless in the dark, I felt I was losing every essential, productive, and meaningful part of my life.

There was comfort in my husband's arms, and I felt extremely grateful that he had been the one to tell me our son was dead. No one except Allen had ever loved Zachary as I did, and no one other than he would ever know exactly how it felt to lose our child. We would now be bonded forever in that way, seared together by a common pain, and each capable of giving a unique comfort because of it.

Twenty-one years ago as dreamy high school sweethearts from Christian homes, we had promised to be married "for better or for worse." We had enjoyed many years of "better"; now we had reached the unimagined "worse." I had enough life experience to know that men and women handle stress differently and that any stress, particularly resulting from a child's death, can take its toll on a marriage. I had heard the warnings and seen the statistics and knew already that Satan was devising a plan to destroy our marriage with this tragedy. I may have lost my son, but I absolutely refused to lose my husband.

In the privacy of our darkened bedroom, on the evening of this darkest day, we held on to each other and made a sacred commitment that was as binding as the marriage vows we took so many years ago with youthful bliss. Somehow knowing that such a promise was vital to our future, we committed that night, without ceremony or fanfare, to endure Zachary's death together with mutual support and communication. We would figure out how to survive this horrific catastrophe one minute, one hour, and one day at a time and would not poison our marriage with blame or finger-pointing. Instinctively knowing we would be far stronger together than we could ever be apart, we promised to bear each other's burdens and not contribute to them. We would love each other and do our best to be strong for our children, for in the days to come, they would desperately be needing the security of two parents in harmony. With many sincere promises, I gasped through my tears and choked on sorrow's intimacy, all the while grateful that I was not alone.

Nothing in my past could have prepared me for this storm and now was not the time to read the directions and assemble a lifeboat. There was no time to frantically dust off the misplaced compass or look up some verse of Scripture memorized as a child and forgotten. There was no time to study theology or cram for this exam. We had either built our foundation upon a rock like the wise man or upon the sinking sands that would soon be washed out from under us.

Everything in my life leading up to this one event had become the training for it. All that I had been taught through the years, gleaned from experience, and learned from Scripture would now be scrutinized, evaluated, and tested against this confusing tragedy. Whatever I had been believing in the daylight, I would now have to believe in the dark. This one life-changing event would either make me shake my fist and turn my back to God, or it would cause me to run to Him and cling with trust to His eternal promises.

The challenge had begun for both Allen and me. Were we ready for this test?

The long hours of darkness brought no logic, no answers. There was only disbelief and terror. My blankets failed to cocoon me in security or offer the comfort they had promised when I was a child. How could I relax, feeling safe and sound in my bed, when my own child wasn't safe and sound in his?

The loss was not just that Zachary had died, it was that something within him wanted to die. I wept for him and for his pain; I wept for me and mine. With the hands of the clock barely moving, the night was long and fitful. We did little more than lie in our bed and weep, closing our eyes only long enough to wipe away the sobbing tears that would not stop.

Dear God,

I do not know what is ahead for me, nor do I in any way know what this death will mean or become. I am not very strong; I am not even brave. I am missing Zachary already, so all I can do is trust in Your faithful goodness and in the power of Your unfailing love.

3

THE WOODS

I have set the L<small>ORD</small> always before me.
Because he is at my right hand,
I will not be shaken.

Psalm 16:8

It was very early Saturday morning when I thought I heard a faint knock on the front door. It seemed much too early for a normal neighborly visit, and I couldn't imagine who would be coming to see me at this hour. Stepping out onto the porch, disheveled and exhausted from lack of sleep, I was pleased to see a dear friend standing there with a look of deep concern on her face.

"I heard on the church prayer chain. I don't know what to do or say," she stammered with wide eyes. "I just came."

I told her what I knew from the night before, which wasn't much. She was full of disbelief that Zachary had killed himself, as was I. We stood and talked a little, and then after a long embrace, this friend slipped away into the early morning coolness to return to her family.

I deeply treasured that she had been the first one to show up and approach our home. However fearful, ill equipped, or unprepared she felt, she set those feelings aside and came. Empty handed, and with a heart full of love and deep concern, this friend taught me a vital lesson about life and loss—just show up.

After she left, on this first morning without my son, there was only one place I wanted to be. I mustered the courage and braved my fears to head in the direction of the woods. Embarking into a past I had no power to change, I walked until our yard ended and then stopped. Taking a deep earthy breath, I stepped into the woods to begin my journey to the site of my child's self-destruction.

The forest was cool and damp, sustaining mystery and secrets, more full of life than death. Spiderwebs sparkled delicately, showing off dewy morning masterpieces. Tiny ferns were gently unrolling themselves, and little animals scuttled away to their hiding places. The children loved traipsing along these paths, chasing and hiding from each other and looking for animal nests and paw prints. They spent hours exploring, searching for old treasures, and making forts with surplus building materials.

We had purchased this property to give our children a more abundant childhood, yet the irony struck me how in the end these woods had provided Zachary with a private place to carry out his final wish. How could something so beautiful have been used in such an ugly way?

What was Zachary agonizing over in those last moments as he prepared to carry out his fatal plan? What was he struggling with as he balanced precariously on the fence between life and death and with this choice lying solely in his hands?

I walked slowly, picking my way over tree roots and pushing aside thorny underbrush, observantly looking around me for anything out of the ordinary. Here in these woods, Zachary had happened upon dead animals, had ceremoniously buried dead pets, and had quite naturally looked death in the face. What had he felt when he saw a dead squirrel or a dead bird? What had he felt when he cradled the stillness of a cold puppy or shoveled cool, damp earth over its body? What does a child even know of death?

Zachary had enjoyed reading heroic books about boys who got lost in the woods and survived the perils of nature by eating berries, rubbing sticks together to start a fire, and studying the stars to find their way back home. He admired those characters that bravely endured plane crashes, persevered after shipwrecks, and survived natural disasters. Why didn't he fight just as hard to get out of these woods alive? He had never been a quitter or a pessimist. Why couldn't he triumph over whatever personal adversity he was facing?

Moving through the woods, I passed a massive old tree that lay fallen on its side. Its gnarled roots stuck out awkwardly in the air leaving a gaping wound in the ground below. Zachary had been violently torn out of my heart in a catastrophic way, leaving a cavernous wound. How would I ever survive this void? Could such a wound even heal?

Walking on, I recognized "the place" in the distance and felt the pounding of my heart escalate. My eyes locked on this sacred spot until finally I arrived where my son had been found lying on the ground. I met Zachary's death at the base of an old tree. Here my own child had lived his last moment, made his last choice, and taken his last breath. Here my little boy struggled with life and lost it to death. Falling to my knees so that my body touched the very place where his had last been, I curled up with my hands covering my face and sobbed from the deepest place of my heart. The emotion was overwhelming to be lying on this place where Zachary shot himself, this place where his precious blood spilled and mixed in with the woodsy dirt. I wanted to stretch my arms and scoop up all of the loose earth, gather it close to my chest, and cling to every piece.

How could my son be dead? He was just learning to live.

Did he die boldly and fearlessly, fully believing that this decision made perfect sense, or was his pounding heart full of terror and doubt? Was he crying? Was he angry? Did he wish someone would show up to stop him?

If only I had arrived home earlier, I would have done everything in my power to help him—had I known he was in danger. I would have wrapped my arms around him and begged him to take a deep breath to clear his mind, all the while reminding him that we all have hurdles to overcome, problems to solve, and obstacles to conquer.

I would have told Zachary that there was a light at the end of this tunnel, that there was a finish line at the end of the race, that the sun would rise again, and that God was stronger than the whirlpool he was spinning in. I would have told him that he'd feel better in the morning, that his broken heart would mend, and that our love for him was deeper than the murky quicksand that was pulling him under. Moving mountains to help him find a solution, I would have laid down my life to protect him from taking his.

What if Zachary had changed his mind midcourse and walked back to the house with that gun still loaded? Although deeply concerned, we would not have thought less of him for what he was planning to do. There would be no dishonor, for although he had fallen, he could get back up, and there would be no shame in the falling. Relieved and grateful to find him alive, we would have vowed to help him find a solution to his problems.

A sound among the trees caused me to look up with curiosity, and as I did, there was a sudden movement behind me. I quickly jumped up to see the swift flash of a white tail as a small deer darted back into the thick brush. Had it been standing there quietly with me all along? Remarkably, during the seven years we had lived on this property, we had seen only two deer in our small woods, and now, on the morning after my son died and near the place of his death, one appeared.

I felt God's presence and immediately thought of Abraham, his immense love for his beloved son Isaac and the agonizing sacrifice this obedient man of God had been asked to make. I envisioned the knife blade lifted high, steel glinting in the sun, when suddenly there was a lamb bleating in the entangled thicket and God's voice shouting, "No, do not carry out this task!"

I had the same God Abraham had—a God who, as a kind and protective parent, is always present in the lives of His children and who actively reminds and encourages each of us to use our free will to choose the path of wisdom and life.

I believed with all my heart that this very same deer had been in the woods the day prior when my own son was preparing to die. Zachary had appreciated deer, had often sketched them, and had even gone hunting several times. Was God trying to distract him from his next move with the appearance of that beautiful animal? Was it indeed a sacrificial lamb waiting in the thicket as a surprise, a diversion, or maybe even a target? Did Zachary even see it? If only he had looked up from his plan and been shaken back into the hopeful beauty around him. If only he had ended that deer's life in exchange for his own.

I wished I had been there when he died. I wished I could have held him, comforted him, and loved him as he took his last breaths, just as surely as I did when he took his first. Instead he died without the comfort of any family member in the solitude of the woods. As his heart slowed its beating, as the blood ceased to flow through his beautiful body, and as he got colder and colder, he died all by himself. The sadness of it all brought choking tears. Isn't that what an old worn out dog does, instinctively limps into the woods to quietly fade away? Alone?

I do not know how long I sat there under the sturdy old trees, but I felt compelled to stay. I turned my eyes upward to study their intricate branches and noticed birds gladly sang and found safety there. I wondered if Zachary had looked at these same trees just yesterday with his artist's eye, had heard the forest music around him, or noticed that the buds were greening on the little bushes sprinkled throughout the woods. I wondered what he thought as he inhaled that woodsy air one last time. Focused solely and bitterly on the present, had he forgotten the countless joys of the past or the unlimited dreams for the future?

In his last tormented moments, had he turned around in second thought or considered that his life had a second chance? Had he glanced back at that big white farmhouse and thought of the warmth and security there or envisioned the faces of the many family members who loved him?

There was one consolation. Zachary's heart was devoted to God and he was now with the One who loved him most, for all along, he had been more God's child than mine. As soon as he took his last look at these beautiful woods, then closed his eyes and ended his life, I fully believe that he went straight into the arms of Jesus. There upon blinking and opening his eyes to view the new and spectacular place where he had just arrived, he set his gaze for the first time upon his glorious heavenly Father. I'd like to think that God kindly put his arms around Zachary, and then with tender comfort and reassurance, explained what had just happened. Any shame or sorrow that my son felt for what he had just done was quickly forgiven. Every confusing trouble was easily explained and all truth was revealed. Pain evaporated. Peace filled my son's heart.

Finally I rose to my feet, and taking one last look at this peaceful forest, I noticed the dappled sunlight dancing and swaying among the moving shadows of the tree branches. At this place, Zachary's own life, so full of sunlight and promise, had wavered and fluctuated among the shadows of darkness. Here in this beautiful place so full of tender spring growth, my son had lost heart and faith. He had lost his way; he had lost his life.

I could stay no longer. Zachary was dead. It was too cruel to be true.

Dear God,

You are not to blame for what happened here in this lovely place. You were sad to watch these tragic events unfold but not in the least bit surprised or taken off guard. How can my beautiful child be dead? If only I could turn back time.

4

RECALLING THE PAST

*The name of the L*ORD *is a strong tower;*
the righteous run to it and are safe.

Proverbs 18:10

Stepping back into the quiet house, I was pleased that the children were still sleeping, for I had work to do. Our friends and family would be getting into cars and climbing aboard airplanes to be with us. Some were coming from great distances with full suitcases and heavy hearts. Others would be arriving from within our small rural farming community, bringing many questions along with their warm casseroles.

All of these loved ones were coming for a funeral, and although I knew nothing about planning one, I was quite certain that Zachary's memorial service would need a video presentation of his life. Sensing that this project was of utmost importance on this first morning without my son, I immediately pulled out the photo albums I had created for Zachary as he was growing up.

I stacked the albums on the kitchen table in chronological order. Starting with the baby pictures, I began flipping through them, pulling out the photos I treasured most.

On November 7, 1992, at 1:50 p.m., we had welcomed our second son into the world—a healthy baby boy weighing ten pounds, two ounces. Looking into his tiny, endearing face, we fell in love, fully knowing that this baby was a gift from above to treasure. Zachary was such a contented, happy baby that his easy personality quickly earned him the name Sunshine.

Turning the pages of the photo album, the sweet chubby baby sucking his thumb turned into an angelic toddling blond holding a beloved white stuffed bunny. Every charming physical milestone was met with the exaggerated, honest cheers that proud parents are known for. Soon Zachary was a cheerful skipping three-year-old in little blue Velcroed sneakers who loved Matchbox cars, Play-Doh, and coloring pictures. With a sweet-natured, compliant spirit and brilliant smile, he spent his preschool years happily sandwiched between two brothers who were his best friends and constant playmates.

The pile of photos grew quickly as Zachary's childhood unfolded. The pictures captured homemade plays, missing teeth, and picnics in the park. They documented him coloring Easter eggs, opening new LEGO sets on his birthday, choosing pumpkins in autumn fields, and decorating Christmas sugar cookies. Sparkling clean in formal Christmas portraits, ready for frontier action in his fringed cowboy vest, or soaking wet from playing in the puddles, Zachary was almost always surrounded by his family. Lingering quickly at each memory, it pained me now to look into each precious face.

This little boy grew up and killed himself?

The house around me was now stirring as the children awakened. On and on, the boy in the photos grew up sturdy and strong, leaving his preschool years behind. His face beamed as he held puppies, raked autumn leaves, played in the sprinkler, made castles in the sand, and sang earnestly at Christmas programs. He was a true delight to everyone who knew him.

Eager and curious, Zachary quickly became an excellent homeschooled student. He enjoyed reading, was an excellent speller, and had the prettiest handwriting I had ever seen. He made us laugh by signing his name with an exclamation point.

I continued to pull my favorite photos from the sleeves, many of which documented a simple childhood in the country. Zachary was all boy, loved riding his bike or rollerblading, and always wanted to be outside. He spent hours with his brothers playing in the woods, building forts, digging holes, and making bows and arrows out of tree saplings. He enjoyed summer fireworks, imaginary sword fights, and building many good campfires. My fingers caressed each photo, coming to rest on the blond hair, sun-bleached from summer play.

A fun-loving prankster who enjoyed a good joke, Zachary took pleasure in playing with water balloons, performing magic tricks, and happily sneaking around the house in the evening to give someone a good scare. Although his two little sisters were often the targets of his endless teasing, Zachary had an infectious cheerfulness and truly embraced life.

The morning passed steadily as I savored each photo. I stacked the books I'd worked through and continued to reach for more. Sometimes there was a shadow behind my shoulder, and I'd turn to see Allen or the older children staring deeply and quietly, searching the face in the photos. The energetic moments now frozen in time portrayed such unmistakable joy and happiness. Where was that happiness now? The irony was unmistakable. How could so much living have ended up in death? How could such eagerness for life have resulted in a desire to die?

I went through the photo albums for hours, forfeiting my morning coffee and a shower. Lost, deep in the days of the past, I was unusually oblivious to the phone's occasional ringing and the normal activity of the household. My son was now dead, and all I wanted to do was hold these photos of his life in my hands.

I turned more pages to see Zachary reaching his teenage years with a gentle and sensitive mellowness. This handsome teenager remained a bright and careful student who loved to read. He enjoyed writing stories as well as taking pictures and playing the piano. He had a gifted mind and a perceptive appreciation for beauty and detail. He loved to play paintball and grilled our hamburgers every Saturday night. Although he enjoyed making his family laugh by reciting hilarious lines from movies and cracking us up with his funny voices, he was not a clown in public. Content to let others be the center of attention, he became more thoughtful, cared for the needs of others, and spent time developing his drawing skills.

Finally as the clock approached midday, the kitchen table was completely covered with mounds of photos. I closed the last book and sadly folded my hands on its cover. I sighed and noticed how hard my chair was.

There would be no more photo albums, no more pages to turn, no more chapters in Zachary's story here on earth. The piles spread before me represented a life that Zachary had seemed to enjoy. It was a simple life, a normal life. There had been joys and achievements. There had been challenges and disappointments, but nothing in any of these photos in any way foreshadowed his suicide or indicated things would end so tragically. I had spent sixteen years caring for Zachary's happiness. With affirmation and encouragement, I sought to raise a godly child who knew Jesus and cared about the needs of others. I had done my best to love and treasure him as my son, yet no measure of love had been enough to keep Zachary alive.

What had happened?

Sadness and fatigue overwhelmed me. The boy in these pictures was dead.

Dear God,

You hear my cries for help and my pleas for understanding. Please wrap Your arms around me and enfold me in the comfort of Your great love, for You never abandon those who search for You nor ignore their cries for help.

5

HIS ROOM

Those who know your name will trust in you,
*for you, L*ORD*, have never forsaken those who seek you.*

Psalm 9:10

I felt an urgency to find the reason for Zachary's death and was determined to have answers ready for the many questions that would be asked by our arriving friends and relatives. So far, I had none.

Believing the answer to his death must be somewhere among the things of his life, I opened the door to Zachary's room on that first day without him and stood in the doorway watching the sunlight stream onto the pine floor. The room was so typical of a teenage boy. There were Star Wars posters on the wall and a burgundy plaid comforter on a neatly made bed. The bookshelf was proudly topped with assembled LEGO sets and neatly filled with classics by C. S. Lewis and J. R. R. Tolkien. Zachary's desk contained tenth-grade schoolbooks, a calculator, and a wallet, while sunglasses, an iPod, and a tiny knife had been tossed onto his dresser. Neatly packed bins contained drawing books, a foreign coin collection, computer games, and the digital camera that Zachary loved to use for creating little movies.

These things were all once held by Zachary's hands, treasured and enjoyed, used with passion and purpose. I touched them tenderly with my fingers, knowing that his would never use them again. Many items had been longed and saved for or received as gifts from people who loved him. Now each of the articles lay still, motionless where they had been placed, like pieces of a museum exhibit that had been roped off with red cord to be forever frozen in time.

What had happened here in this room where he lived, where he did so much pondering, and where he perhaps even doubted the value of living?

I opened the closet and flipped through his limp clothes, running my fingertips over the items I had washed and folded so many times. Inhaling his smell, I wistfully touched jeans, T-shirts, sweatshirts, and a few winter jackets that I now wanted to slip around my shoulders. The top shelf held a baseball cap, knitted hats, and winter gloves, while sneakers, tan suede work boots, and slippers were strewn about the floor. These were the clothes he had worked and played in, clothes I told him he looked handsome in, clothes he had been alive in.

I pawed through the garbage can, hating to inspect my son's trash, hating the feeling of invading my son's privacy. I saw only candy wrappers, scribbles of old math problems, and used tissues. I found no clues or surprises, nothing shocking or disturbing. Even under his bed, there were no monsters, no revelations. I saw only one dirty sock, an old softball, and a little red Matchbox car.

Walking around his room, I picked up a drawing pencil from his desk and rolled it slowly between my fingers. There were stacks of sketchbooks filled with pencil drawings Zachary had created and proudly signed using his middle name, Lee. I had given each of these extraordinary sketches lavish praise when he had proudly showed them to me—I had even rescued discarded crumpled drawings from the trash. I flipped through one sketchbook and admired his fine pencil strokes on cabins and trees, imagining the time that went into such precision. I studied the shading and shadowing on animals and landscapes, examining details the way his insightful eyes might have seen them. Careful not to smudge any of Zachary's beautiful, serene artwork with my tears, I wept for his talent and for his appreciation of peaceful things. Laying the sketchbook tenderly back in its place, I knew I was his biggest fan.

I picked up an envelope and counted several hundred dollars. Always looking for a way to make a buck, Zachary faithfully held a few weekly mowing jobs and did regular yard work for neighbors. I slipped my hands into his heavy work gloves, bringing them to my face to inhale the fragrance of the leather mixed with his scent. He was such a great help with all of the weeding and mowing around the house and often could be seen moving dirt or gravel with a wheelbarrow. He received both pleasure and pride from washing our cars and took initiative with extra jobs that we paid him to complete. He counted his money with great excitement, prideful of the work he had done and happily anticipating his next purchase.

For a moment I held Zachary's Bible against my chest and wondered about the wisdom he gleaned from Scripture's teachings. Zachary had been saved when he was five, baptized when he was eleven, and had read through his entire Bible when he was fourteen. He memorized many Bible verses, including several complete chapters. What had the messages in God's Word meant to my son?

What had the Holy Spirit revealed as Zachary tried to glean wisdom and understanding from its pages?

Hadn't we taught our son that God loved him and had a plan for his life? Hadn't we taught him that God was not yet finished with his story and that wonderful and exciting things lay hidden in the unwritten chapters? I thought the main goal of Christian parenting was to teach our children to transfer their love and dependence on us to devotion and reliance on God. Had I failed in this one task I set out to accomplish?

I ran my fingers through a box of rocks that Zachary had collected, each with a unique shape, a fascinating color, or an interesting texture. He had selected these for their beauty or uniqueness—because they were different from the ordinary—and then given them a treasured status. I wondered if Zachary felt different from other people. He was so extraordinary to me, but did he value the traits he saw in himself that made him unique from others?

I now studied his room, trying to see it as Zachary had, trying desperately to see life as my son had seen it. What had living looked like through his eyes? What had he perceived from his reality?

My eyes came to rest on Zachary's bed just as surely as his precious body had rested there. I envisioned him lying in the darkness and looking up at the ceiling before he drifted off to sleep each night. I wondered what he thought about as he closed his eyes, what he grappled with as he tried to untangle the struggles of his life. Is this where he first started to think of death? Is this where he mulled it over in his mind ambivalently, tossing around the dreadful idea indecisively?

I considered the fact that sixteen years ago Zachary had been handed to me in the hospital as a tiny, unfamiliar stranger. Now, in many ways, it seemed he had left me as a stranger as well. For even though I had come to deeply know and understand my son and could now look around this room and recognize physical things that defined him, I realized in an empty way that everything I truly understood about Zachary paled in comparison to something very vital I never even knew.

I closed the door in utter sadness, closed the door to my son's life.

No one knew him anymore.

Dear God,

What happened? What did I miss? Mysteries lie within the hearts of the people I love, and they are seen and understood by You alone. I take refuge under the wings of the Almighty, for I am lost. I greatly loved this child.

6

SHARING AT CHURCH

Guard my life and rescue me;
let me not be put to shame,
for I take refuge in you.
May integrity and uprightness protect me,
because my hope is in you.

Psalm 25:20–21

If people in society are afraid of natural death, then they are clearly terrified of suicide. I couldn't fault them. Suicide crosses a forbidden boundary and is a blatant trespass against the unwritten rules of society that state people are, after all, not supposed to choose where and how they will die. Since self-preservation and self-survival are basic human instincts, the thought of someone killing himself is processed by the mind as appalling and ghastly. It is a noble idea that all members of society are supposed to fight for life, not end it. Even wounded warriors on the battlefield cry out for life. Suicide unsettles the comfortable feelings we thought we had about ourselves, others, God, and the workings of human society in general.

Suicide now lived in my house as surely as my son did not. It was a scandalous, dirty word to me, an unclean taboo full of fearful stigma, a social leprosy of repulsion and terror. In my naïve mind, suicide had always been a dishonorable method of death associated with those who were in trouble or who had no one to love them and nowhere to turn. Suicide wasn't a word to be associated with a treasured child loved by his siblings, adored by his parents, and cherished by his relatives. It wasn't a word to be linked with a kind, talented child who had tremendous gifts to offer the world. Yet now that ghastly word was in my daily vocabulary and had already rolled off my tongue far too many times. Shame on me for my smug and arrogant assumptions. Shame on me for my ignorant and misinformed criticism.

Generally within a family unit, a suicide doesn't occur without it reflecting poorly on the members left behind. Since happy people do not kill themselves and normal, well-adjusted people who are "in their right minds" do not end their own lives, it is assumed that difficulties existed prior to the event. Zachary's suicide boldly announced that serious problems were present in our family, whether we were aware of them or not. Suicide produces murmurs from family members, horror from old friends, and disbelief from close friends who are simply too shocked to speak. The family members who are left behind get scrutinized, questioned, and sometimes blamed for their loved one's unnatural death.

Was our entire family now guilty by association? Did our relationships with Zachary imply involvement or fault? My character felt permanently tarnished, my reputation stained, and my identity colored. I was exposed as an inadequate parent; Zachary was exposed as a troubled child.

A troubled child? How could that be?

I acknowledged myself to be a blessed woman, glowing in a happy marriage, and filled with contentment as I homeschooled my large family in a thoughtfully restored farmhouse. For many years, we had fostered abused and neglected children and were preparing to adopt two preschoolers needing a family. I shopped at garage sales, tended my tomatoes, and often filled our kitchen with the aroma of warm bread. I loved the slow pace of my wonderful life and treasured spending my days with the children.

While some around me struggled with financial difficulties, bad marriages, and discontented lives, I repeatedly gave God credit for every blessing Allen and I held dear. We had worked hard for the things we enjoyed, and I did not take my marriage nor family for granted.

Had I believed, in the back of my mind, that an appreciation for my blessings ensured I would be exempt from pain? Had I believed that my trust in God and devotion to my family would protect me from sorrow?

Despite the raised eyebrows of some, I was confident of my values and pleased with what I had accomplished in life. I knew we were deemed by some to be a nontraditional family and wondered now if these characteristics defining our family's uniqueness were magnified against Zachary's death, for when a suicide happens—something that is so out of the ordinary and so rarely heard of—people could not be blamed for drawing their conclusions that bizarre and odd things happen to strange and peculiar families.

Having seen my own misunderstandings about suicide, I now feared the misinformation and confusion beginning to travel throughout our community grapevine. Vague, cautious announcements were spreading that "Zachary LaBonte had died unexpectedly," and the distorted message circulating through the church prayer chain had simply stated, "Zachary had an accident at home and it was fatal."

I knew I needed to set the record straight.

Having nothing to hide and unafraid to speak the truth, just two days after Zachary's death, I slipped into church on Sunday morning right before it was time for the service to conclude with prayer requests and announcements. I waited quietly in the back until it was time for sharing, and then with adrenaline pulsing in my ears, I walked slowly up one of the aisles to the front of the room. I heard quiet gasps and nervous shifting among the chairs.

I stood at the front of the church in complete silence as the crowd looked up at me expectantly waiting for the truth. My mouth was dry and my hands were clammy. I swallowed, stared at the microphone, and wondered what to say first. My son had been dead less than two days. What was I doing here? Wasn't this story far too personal and far too painful to share like this on a public stage? I felt a chill in the room and heard my heart beating loudly in my chest.

Suicide is paralyzing terror and sends a chilling shiver. I felt it in my soul and saw it before me in these faces.

Our family's reaction to this frightful death was being studied, and I hoped that sharing our story would ease the awkwardness and stigma that were already and inevitably growing like wild, rambling roadside weeds. Maybe I could teach people how to relate both to me and to others who would have this awful experience in the future. Perhaps my guilt-ridden heart also hoped that by being honest and transparent, I could prevent the blame of Zachary's death from being placed on me.

Finally, I took a deep breath and looked out into the faces of the crowd. There were tears everywhere. This church family loved my son and had enjoyed watching him grow up. They had seen Zachary as a regular fixture in Bible school and youth group. They had watched him willingly move chairs, clear tables, and assist with children's programs. Faithfully each week he ran the overhead projector that displayed the songs and sermon notes and was recently learning to run the audio equipment. Zachary was a vital part of this church family and had blessed many people throughout the years with his calm and peaceful spirit.

The love of the emotional congregation before me mustered my courage and I began to speak, telling Zachary's story the best I could. I shared what I knew and requested prayers for our family concerning this staggering journey we had been forced to embark on. When I was done speaking, the pastors laid hands on my shoulders and prayed. After they finished, the service concluded and I walked to the back of the sanctuary where a loving line quickly formed. Many dear friends eagerly came to offer their sympathy, and I gratefully received the rich compassion and true Christian love of those who truly cared and shared in our family's sorrow.

Dear God,

Thank You for these dear ones who loved Zachary, for we are all enriched for knowing him. My tears do not stop. Please infuse me with a tremendous strength so that I can show the world Your power through me.

7

FUNERAL HOME

Answer me when I call to you,
O my righteous God.
Give me relief from my distress;
be merciful to me and hear my prayer.

Psalm 4:1

Allen and I had a Sunday afternoon appointment at the funeral home. The drive was a beautiful little trip through winding country roads boasting old houses, beautiful barns, and pastures filled with calmly grazing animals. Reminiscent of a leisurely drive or a casual laid-back errand, I would have enjoyed the peaceful scenic views on any other day.

But not today. Zachary was dead. I was heading to a funeral home, a place I knew nothing about. I was heading down a staggering journey that I was totally unfamiliar with. We were confused, and our moods mirrored the lack of peace in our hearts. How could a strong and peaceful sixteen-year-old with a promising future have been thinking about death? How could his bright and gifted mind have made such a terrible decision that brought me now to this grim place?

As I got out of the car, my legs felt like lead. Where was I, and what was I doing here? Everything within my heart and mind wanted to deny, refuse, and reject this place. But I was a mother, required to cope. I bit my lip and tasted blood.

Our pastor met us at the entrance, and we walked silently into the low, darkened building. The air was stuffy and filled with a stale smell I didn't recognize. There were heavy red curtains drawn shut at every window that matched the gaudy red carpeting on the floor. Formal wing chairs in the foyer were the only thing that looked familiar or seemed appropriate in this foreign place.

I was strangely aware that I looked like a battle casualty for there was a wounded aura about me that even I detected. This was received with kind, gentle handshakes and sympathetic whispers as the funeral director led us into a small, quiet room and seated us at a polished wooden table where we nervously began to make arrangements for our son's burial.

We were told that the body had been autopsied and would be returned to the funeral home on Monday, the next day. Had we thought about where we wanted to bury the body? what kind of casket we wanted for the body? how we wanted to dress the body? care for the body?

I immediately felt hot irritation rising within my chest and wanted to shout, "Yes! I have spent my entire life thinking about how to care for his body! Furthermore—" I wanted to yell, as the scorching fury rose like molten lava erupting from a volcano, "my son's name is Zachary, not the body!"

But I was silent as the many questions began. Which cemetery would we like to use? Did we want a private family burial? or a formal church service? How did we want the obituary to be worded? Had we thought about music? Would we like to rent candelabras? What kind of sermon would we prefer? Did we want to order a guest book, candles, and thank-you cards as well?

As innocent as the necessary questions were, turmoil hammered at my chest, heat throbbed in my face. This was outrageous! What cemetery would I "like" to use? What kind of casket do I "want"? What kind of sermon would I "prefer"? The horror tightened its grip on my throat and I could not breathe. There was simply no air.

I wanted to holler and throw a temper tantrum, "I would not like to use a cemetery! I don't care about ornamental candelabras, decorative candles, or elegant guest books! I do not WANT any funeral service or any sermon, and I especially do not WANT a casket for my little boy!"

Incredibly frustrated, I focused on the blinking of my eyes, because it was the only movement in my entire body. I hid my face by glancing through the brochure we had been given. I heard the funeral director, this same man who had put his hands on my son's dead body, explain the benefits of package A versus the merits of package B. I felt as if I were purchasing a new vehicle. Noticing the final line where the grand total would go, it seemed hideous that we were going through this tragedy, and on top of all that, we would be charged for it! Outrageous! We would have to pay for this horrible experience? Don't people only get billed for things in life that they choose, like fine dinners, new cars, and hotel reservations?

My eyes burned with frustration, and I sat like a traumatized, frightened child who needed repetition and explanation. I managed to blankly assist Allen in answering the funeral director's questions concerning our wishes until I finally became completely overwhelmed

and could no longer keep my composure. I put my head down on
the shiny table and heard deep sobs I didn't recognize as my own. I
was surprised by the intensity of my emotion but did not care who
heard. My little boy was dead. I wanted to spit out the bitter taste
in my mouth. Was this nightmare really happening? Someone please
turn this horror movie off.

God had promised never to give me more than I could handle.
Had He overestimated my abilities? Had He slipped up and
accidentally given me more than I could manage?

By some miracle, my maternal instincts kicked in. I felt a jolt of
power and sat up straight, willing myself to concentrate. As Zachary's
mother, I had always tried to do the right things at the right time. I
required it now of myself to give my best effort to make these vital
decisions, purposing to take care of my child in death as surely as I
had in life.

I helped Allen supply information to questions I had never once
pondered and discussed lists of details concerning our selections for
the burial and funeral. For the last matter of business, we dictated
the obituary that contained far too few facts about Zachary's life
and even fewer specifics about how much he meant to each of us.
Our child's entire life was now briefly summarized in a few concise
paragraphs in a hometown newspaper. After more handshakes and
whispers, we speechlessly got into our car. Wondering in the end if
any of our decisions were right, I concluded that I had never before
made a purchase that I was so regretfully unsure of.

Driving home past the same scenic pastures full of serenely
grazing animals, Allen and I looked at each other now and then. It
was surreal. I kept wondering if it was true that we had just spent
an hour and a half at a funeral home on this bright and cloudless

Sunday afternoon making burial arrangements because our sixteen-year-old son was now dead.

Dear God,

I can barely breathe and terror grips my heart, for this experience is horrible and unfamiliar. I am uneducated in such things and frightened by what I do not know. I have much to learn, but do not know where to start. Please help me.

8

I AM LOVED

We also ought to love one other.... But if we love one another,
God lives in us and his love is made complete in us.

1 John 4:11–12

On Monday morning, the spring daffodils pompously bloomed. Hadn't I been standing peacefully on my porch just three days ago waiting for this display? The golden beauties had unfolded their tender buds and straightened themselves to reveal their brilliance to the world. It was ironic to see such budding beauty, such blossoming potential, when the life of a strong, vibrant teenager had violently ended. It was a mockery to have such miraculous wonder in our yard when there was such raw pain in our hearts. I watched the flowers bob in the spring breeze and thought about the harsh, dark winter they had just come through. The metaphor was not lost. I wished Zachary had also held on through his darkness, held on long enough to bloom.

Inside the house, we were not celebrating spring's gift of new life. There was a flurry of activity. Beautiful flower arrangements were being delivered, cars came and went, and the phone rang constantly.

For two days, our extended family and dear friends had been arriving. Canceling their appointments and dropping the week's agenda, they came from near and far with sympathy and love. How it comforted us to feel their warm, familiar arms around us. How it lifted some of the burden to look into their faces and see them mirror our own inability to comprehend this devastating crisis.

Tossing their purses aside and rolling up their sleeves, delaying their own lunches and ignoring their jet lag, these dear loved ones came to serve our family. They did not wait for an assignment, but plunged right in, humbling themselves to meet any need they noticed. They took over the ironing, thrust their hands into soapy dishwater, and took out the garbage. Others went shopping, lists in hand, for practical essentials we needed in the house as well as for items we requested for the funeral.

I gratefully let these loved ones take care of me and my home. I let them answer the phone, take out my garbage, and stack the food in my refrigerator. I let them fold my clean clothes, sweep the floors, feed the dogs, and wash my children's sticky fingers. Stunned, I sat back in appreciation for this army of loving volunteers, amazed that these menial tasks were so cheerfully completed.

Favorite uncles playfully kept the mood light while loving aunts reliably nurtured and doted. Cousins chased and squealed while grandparents sat back taking it all in. Teenagers competed at board games and munched on snacks as adults caught up on each other's lives. Although we were together for a sad occasion, the mood almost resembled a family reunion, and it soothed my heart to hear the happy banter.

The news of our tragedy seemed to have set off an instinct in the minds of our church friends, co-workers, and neighbors. Knowing that providing meals would meet our needs, their wringing restless hands got busy purchasing groceries and kindly preparing food for our family. Praying for us as they chopped and stirred, they lovingly created food in their own kitchens to bring us comfort in ours.

The food arrived in large pans with quantities to conquer the hunger of vast numbers of people. We received homemade bread to nourish us, cheesy casseroles to soothe us, and steaming Crock-Pots of soup to dissolve the lumps in our throats. The counters filled with fresh fruit, homemade cookies, and tall, layered cakes with thick icing that seemed more appropriate for a birthday celebration than a teenager's funeral. The fridge bulged with gallons of milk, jugs of juice, and sandwich fixings to take care of us for weeks. There were even bags of chips, sugary breakfast cereals, and ice cream to cheer the children. Our visiting loved ones were not in need of anything, and it pleased me to see my guests and children feasting with such pleasure.

Dear, thoughtful friends brought paper plates, disposable cups, and plastic utensils to free us for more important tasks. Others carried in grocery staples such as toilet paper and tissues to keep the household running smoothly. Delivered with quietly whispered instructions, there was always a sympathetic hug and a kindly whispered, "Call us if you need anything." How grateful we were for every last detail that was thought of at a time when we couldn't think clearly for ourselves nor were in any way capable of knowing what we needed.

Besides bringing food and other necessities, those who loved us met the emotional needs of our family in creative ways. For the children, friends brought stuffed animals to hug, journals to put confusing thoughts into, and movies to keep worried minds occupied. Others brought books, stickers, craft projects, and bubbles to keep various-sized hands busy.

Each baking pan, plate, and bowl that entered our house was a symbol of love. Every overflowing grocery bag to lighten our load and each considerate gift to ease our pain touched my heart in a deep and lasting way. My husband, children, and I were all learning firsthand many enormous lessons about death and the outpouring of community sympathy. We were all humbled and felt deeply loved.

Dear God,

Thank You for our extended family and for a community of believers who serve as the body of Christ. Please bless them for their outpouring of kindness and sacrificial efforts to help carry this tremendous burden. I feel their love.

9

BURYING MY SON

*Jesus said ..., "I am the resurrection and the life. He
who believes in me will live, even though he dies."*

John 11:25

Some in the family were keeping busy with chores as a way of coping
with the shock, while others were bouncing from relative to relative,
eating far too many sweets and spinning in the chaos, totally unsure
of this break in their routine.

I will forever be grateful to our oldest teenage son for producing
Zachary's slide show while simultaneously bearing the vast weight of his
brother's sudden death. For three days and with little help, he worked
his technical magic with a scanner and two computers and skillfully
organized, scanned, and cropped the pile of photos I had pulled from
the photo albums. It was a monumental task, and after adding some
of Zachary's favorite Christian music, the completed project was a true
masterpiece and would become a treasured gift to all who loved Zachary.

We had decided to have the burial on Wednesday afternoon at
four o'clock with a private dinner for family and friends following

the service inside the church, then an open community funeral at seven o'clock. Allen and I, with the help of our older children, were finalizing the graveside service and funeral by choosing praise music, selecting Scriptures, and ordering bulletins. We also were gathering many personal items from Zachary's room to place on tables at the funeral and preparing his yearly school pictures and many of his sketches for presentation.

At last Wednesday afternoon arrived. Somehow we washed our faces, put on clean clothes, and drove to the church parking lot. Was this really happening? How would I cope with this horribly public event? How would I dutifully manage many hours of being the center of attention? I did not like my new role at all.

I got out of the car, trying to believe that my son was dead, wondering when the news would sink in and stop shocking me with its horror. Shutting the passenger door, I caught a glimpse of myself in the mirror and saw a familiar face twisted with pain. Was that really me? I looked like I had been run over by a truck. A week ago I had been young, hopeful, calm, and naïve about many things. Now I felt old and anxious, saddened and heartbroken—as if I had suffered much too deeply for one human being and had already lived far too long for one lifetime.

The sky sagged with grim streaks of gray, and the teasing March winds whipped about as a reminder that winter might not be over after all. Allen and I walked into the cemetery toward a canvas canopy supported by metal legs. I felt a magnetic force but could not tell if I was being drawn nearer or altogether repelled.

Each painful step moved us closer until we reached the small crowd of close friends and family who stood waiting with their own tears of sorrow. I gasped to see Zachary's casket suspended over a deep hole in the ground, for it was an unfamiliar and foreign sight. I could do nothing but stare at that beautiful wooden box that contained the precious body of the soul I loved for sixteen years. A large canvas covered a pile of freshly shoveled earth behind the grave, hiding the inevitable, final component of this last experience in my son's life on earth.

Underneath a bright blue tent, we were directed to folding metal chairs cleverly disguised with matching blue velour that seemed much too flamboyant for this somber occasion. Every emotion was sucked out of me except for passive disbelief, for there was a surreal quality about the ceremony as if I were watching a graveside service from an old black-and-white movie. As I sat uncomfortably on the metal chair, my mind was in a fog and I barely heard the heartfelt voices singing "Amazing Grace" behind me. The pastor's message sounded distorted, his words lost in the wind. I tried to concentrate on the Scripture verses but could only look with vacant eyes at the closed casket just within my reach, thinking only of my son lying still and lifeless there at my knees.

Zachary had been blessed with a strong, healthy body that physically enabled him to do the many things he loved. I imagined him riding his bike, chasing his sisters, mowing the lawn, and roughhousing with his brothers. I closed my eyes, straining and struggling to get the picture just right as I forced myself to recall the color of his eyes, the contour of his back, and the look of his hands. I wished to touch him now, to feel his familiar warm body in one last embrace. I wished I had memorized him better. But he was quiet and still before me now and I sat the same, staring at the beautiful wooden box that would soon go deep into the ground as a last cradle to gently hold the precious silent shell of my beloved little boy.

Finally, after a few more Scripture verses and another prayer, the small crowd stepped out from beneath the canopy, stood in the grass, and released red and white heart-shaped balloons in Zachary's honor. I had hoped the cheerful balloons would slowly float peacefully into the heavens and give the smaller children a measure of comfort and joy, but instead the wild March winds twisted their ribbons together, jerked them chaotically into clusters, and whipped them higher and higher into the sky. The tangled mess seemed fitting.

Our friends and family were dismissed to walk into the church to wait for dinner and then the funeral. Allen, the children, and I remained privately at the gravesite, unmoving, speechlessly staring at the brand-new casket. How sad that its beautiful brown wood would soon be buried in the ground, too quickly appreciated, too quickly admired, just like our son.

The stocky workmen, who had been waiting obscurely on the sidelines, began to work efficiently with their ropes and pulleys as the handsome casket with our beloved boy's body went lower and lower into the dark, into the cold, into eternity. Looking death in the face, the eyes of my children were somber and cheerless. While I could only wonder what this dismal experience was doing to their minds, I was firmly convinced that their hearts were far too small to contain a pain this large.

I had known Zachary as a loving, talented son and was now forced to deal with the loss of my child. The children knew Zachary as their funny, kind brother and would have to come to terms with the death of a beloved sibling, a childhood companion, and a close friend. These children shared parents and bedrooms, hairbrushes and toys, as well as private jokes and unwritten codes of honor.

They shared family celebrations, annual traditions, and doting relatives. They grew into each other's chores and bulky winter coats and graduated one by one into later bedtimes and driving privileges. There were mutual complaints of seemingly unfair parenting behind closed doors and many pacts of secrecy sworn to loyally cover for each other's misdeeds. This trustful confiding in each other as well as the forgiveness from erupting arguments and soaring emotions was the glue that cemented them together.

Zachary had been a part of every defining moment and every significant family memory. He had played a role at each birthday and holiday celebration, each move and family vacation. He had been there for the thrill of Christmas morning, the joy of new pets, and the action of rambunctious snowball fights. He had been present for crazy singing, water-balloon battles, and late night dialogue that went hours past bedtime. During household chores, sibling squabbles, long car rides, and boring rainy afternoons, through thick and thin, amid good or bad, Zachary had been a part of a million simple memories of childhood.

Each sibling saw him in a very different way, each with a unique bond and intricate relationship from which I was quite naturally excluded. This I would always enjoy watching but would probably never fully understand. With Zachary's death, each sibling had lost a part of themselves, a witness to the past, a co-dreamer of the future, and a defining element of who each of them was.

Gone was the pleasure of continuing to grow up with Zachary. Gone were the opportunities for enjoying becoming adults with Zachary, watching each other's families grow, and sharing in the challenges of growing old. My beloved children experienced their first bitter taste of grief. Their innocence had been stolen as well as their youthful confidence in the belief that their family members would always be there for them.

This was not a life experience I wanted for my children. Watching their young faces as their brother was being lowered into the earth, I could only pray that every cheerful memory of Zachary would sink deeply into their hearts with vivid solidity and become more precious as time went on. Although not completely understanding, they were totally capable of sensing our heart-rending agony. Too young to realize what Zachary's death might mean in the future, each, in their own way and at their own level of maturity, seemed to comprehend enough about this tragedy to know this painful death was now a part of our family's life. I hoped the children were learning that no matter what devastation burst into our lives, we would do our best to love, support, and meet each other's emotional needs.

Finally, our family could watch no longer, and in one single moment with a gesture that was powerful and final, Allen took my arm and turned me away from our son's grave. Together and with the children following, we walked away, leaving a part of our hearts six feet under the damp March dirt. We did not look back nor glance over our shoulders, for we knew our time with Zachary was finished. We left him there. Our boy.

We walked into the church and gathered with our immediate family and close friends in the fellowship hall for a beautiful dinner that had been prepared by loving hands within the community. Young cousins and playmates ate their fill and cheerfully laughed while, in a contrast of moods, adults stared at uneaten food, heavy with sadness.

After the meal, our family was taken to a small, private room where we waited for the funeral to begin. My heart pounded as if I were an actor nervously pacing behind the red curtain in anticipation of the opening scene. I was a part of a play I wanted no role in, preparing to stand in front of scenery I did not recognize. Dressed in an ill-fitting costume, I felt embarrassed because I did not know my lines. Finally, with a cue reminiscent of our wedding, Allen, the children, and I walked down the aisle as the congregation searched our faces with sympathetic eyes.

Zachary's suicide had sandblasted me. My soul was without secret. His death had stripped away all pride and confidence to reveal my painful vulnerability to the world. The entire community knew how our son had died. I felt humiliated and completely full of shame over any contribution I might have made to his death. I was convinced that the world saw me as a failure for raising a child who grew up and took his own life. No one wanted to walk in our shoes. No one envied our lives.

But I felt aware that I was teaching my children how to react to death whether I wanted to or not, so I took my place in the front row of Zachary's funeral as bravely as I could. Putting my arms around as many of my children as I could reach and sitting beside the man I loved, I gathered strength from these loved ones as well as from my extended family sitting in the rows behind us. This was my job right now to be here, and I would do it with as much dignity and self-respect as I could muster.

The memorial service was a beautiful celebration of Zachary's life as well as a time of worship to thank God for blessing us with the pleasures and joys of knowing this child. I had been the recipient of much love and will forever cherish the precious, sweet memories of Zachary's childhood. Even if I had known that his life would end in such a tragic way, I wouldn't have traded one day of the last sixteen years. I could be ashamed of the way he died or proud of the life he lived. I felt pride and overwhelming happiness to have known such a wonderful child.

But this glimmer of happiness was quickly doused with horror. Is Zachary really dead? Is this for real that I am sitting in the front row of my sixteen-year-old son's funeral and I will never again hear his voice or see his face? My tears came freely, and I felt no need to stop or hide them. I forced my attention on the extravagant flower arrangements that were lovingly sent in Zachary's honor and let the praise music strengthen and comfort me.

After the service, our entire extended family stood in a receiving line for two hours, feeling comfort from being near the tables that held Zachary's personal possessions and drawing encouragement from the many who came through the line to offer their kind condolences. Numerous church members, neighbors, co-workers, and friends from the foster care and homeschooling communities came with thoughtful sympathies and tearful embraces, showing both tenderness for our family and fond love for our son.

It was very late when the crowd thinned and the lights were systematically turned off one by one in the sanctuary. Feeling very loved, but also emotionally drained from sorrow and sadness, we drove home and walked into our darkened home. Looking at the clock, we suddenly realized how physically exhausted we were.

Everyone else had returned home to their intact families, but here in the quiet house where Zachary lived, our home now felt like a sterile museum full of inanimate objects, for everywhere and in every room, there were reminders of the boy who once lived here. We were overwhelmed once again by the shocking horror of this tragedy and the loneliness of how solely and utterly ours it was.

Zachary was really gone. Really dead. It was an awful truth. I had crossed a burned bridge from one life to another, the embers of which were still scorched and smoldering behind me. How was I supposed to bury my son one day and then wake up the next to make our coffee, fetch our newspaper, feed the cat, and keep on living? Walking up the stairs, I paused in the hallway outside Zachary's room and looked out into the dark night. I was surprised to see the moon and stars—quite amazed actually—to see them still faithfully doing their jobs on this sad, unforgettable night with my son's cold body lying out there in the ground beneath this dark sky. The moon was round and full, brightly glowing and fully complete. I had an eerie sense that my life would never be any of those things again.

Having never lost a loved one, I did not know what *dead* meant. Sheltered and inexperienced in such matters, I had no clue how much there was to learn, neither could I begin to imagine how long such lessons would take. I was innocent and naïve of how deeply human pain could plunge, and it was a blessing of protection that we did not know the entire scope of what Zachary's death would mean to each of us or how it would color everything we saw and did in our lives. Safe behind our cloud of shock, the full impact of the future was veiled. We fell into bed dazed with pain, relieved that this day was finally over.

Dear God,

My child's body is now deep in the ground and our family is no longer intact. I feel fractured and broken, for all my loved ones are not safe and collectively together. You weep alongside us now, and Your weeping brings me comfort.

10

TERRIFIED OF LIVING

Be merciful to me, O LORD, for I am in distress;
my eyes grow weak with sorrow,
my soul and my body with grief.

Psalm 31:9

The next day I awoke totally unsure of how to begin the rest of my life. The funeral was over. Now what?

There was little to do but receive food, take cards and gifts out of the mailbox, answer the phone, and sadly stare at memories in the photo albums. We told our story again and again to those who were just now hearing the news, still unable to comprehend this crisis for ourselves.

Like a wildly spinning tornado that demolishes everything in its path, this death barged into our lives, demanded that everything change, and insisted that no one walk away unscathed. Now the smoke was clearing, the dust was settling, and the debris was becoming crystal clear.

At that one moment when my son's life ended, my new life began. Zachary did not only take his own life, he took part of mine with it. I was now the mother of a child who died by suicide. This wasn't who I planned to be or a role I signed up for. I was absolutely bewildered. How does a mother live when her own child wanted to die? How do I begin the overwhelming task of resuming my life?

I had been so grateful for the company of family and friends who had sacrificed their time to travel and be with us, but now they were packing up and leaving. Thankful for the distraction of having them in our home, I wondered how I would survive without their help and comfort. I dreaded everyone returning to their usual routines while I was left with a life that would never be normal again. I feared being in a silent house with quiet children looking up into my face for cues on how to pick up the shattered pieces of our lives and put them back together.

Yet the last of the company left and just nine days after our child had died, Monday morning came and Allen returned to work. The sun rose in the sky just as it did every single day, and I awoke petrified, just as I had feared.

I used to love mornings. Hearing the birds serenade the world with their cheery wake-up chorus was a promise of a brand-new start. But those days were over, for now when the sun came up, I was in the land of the dark. Far from the safe and familiar, I had been transported into a foreign country and carelessly dropped into an eerie, barren wasteland. The skies here were a deep threatening gray and the landscape dismal and cheerless. Bleak clouds hovered, plaguing me with emptiness. I was a million miles from home.

How would I ever live without Zachary in this odd and unfamiliar world? How would I live the rest of my days carrying around this kind of pain—carrying this knowledge of what my own child had done? How would I get used to an empty chair at the dining room table, an empty seat in the van, an empty spot on the church pew?

The day loomed ahead of me. The week loomed ahead of me. My whole life loomed ahead of me.

The suicide had totally eroded my trust in others, and I obsessively feared for my family. If Zachary had been hopeless enough to kill himself without my foreseeing it, was there a chilling possibility that others in my own home—perhaps even myself—had the lurking capability to do this dark and deadly thing? Were other people I love hopelessly vulnerable to be swept away in a moment of weakness and despair?

Who will I lose next? Will someone else abandon me in death? Will I ever feel safe again? I was holding my breath for another tragedy, suspicious of any impending danger, and fully aware that I had no clue what might be lurking around corners or hiding under rocks. If the unthinkable had already happened, couldn't I be destined for more terror? Wasn't the absurd now within the realm of the possible?

The fearful watchfulness was exhausting. I was forever on edge and braced for the next wave of horror and destruction, like a jittery, terrified soldier on the alert who huddles in a bunker nervously hoping the next dreadful blast of artillery will not land on top of him. Vigilantly on guard against anything that might be awry, I was a watchful sentry, alert for further attacks. I would not be caught off guard again.

I was terrified to leave my children home alone or in the care of somebody else. I panicked every time I called for a child and did not get an immediate answer and repeatedly asked the children where their siblings were. I absolutely could not relax.

I had gauges and meters running all the time on the moods of everyone in the house. I examined and reinspected the needles and numbers to see who seemed happy and who might be depressed. Alarm bells clanged and sirens whistled constantly as I battled the fear I could not shake.

If I sent a child to his room or took away a privilege, would he sulk and plan his own death? If I failed to do as someone wished or declined to buy that child what she wanted, was I being held hostage with her very life in my hands? Was I responsible for everyone's emotional health? Would I be forced to play a part in the further destruction of my family? I felt terrified, vulnerable, and totally out of control.

"I can do all things through Christ who strengthens me" was a Bible concept I learned as a little girl skipping off to Sunday school. Now this simple verse leaped off the pages of my Bible and seemed far more than just a trite cliché. It appeared to be a guarantee sent straight from God. I can do all things? I can even survive this suicide of my own child? I had no idea how, but I had to believe it was true.

Like a fearful child seeking the comfort of a grown-up's lap, I frantically ran to the only sure thing in my life—the unchangeable and loving character of God. He was faithful, and surely He would uphold me with His right arm.

Somehow with a shaky return to normal living, I did my best that Monday and Tuesday, stumbling and tripping into Thursday, Friday, and the next week, relying on God's comforting presence and every piece of my faith that had sustained me in the past. Deep inside, while I worried that life would never get better, I also deeply hoped it would.

As the activity of the house pulled me into action each morning, I managed to put a weak smile on my face and slid back into the habitual ruts of my routine, for the children expected hot meals, clean clothes, and rides to their activities. Focusing on them, my only goal and simplest ambition in life was to stay alive for those who needed me. If I had done that by the end of the day, I counted it a success. Perhaps I could survive the dying by concentrating on the living. This became my prayer and sole motivation. While I wasn't sure that God would ever take my pain away, I was totally convinced that He would faithfully help me bear it.

Dear God,

Terrified and fearful, I have no idea where to place my next footstep. I want to move forward by the light of Your Word, which is a lamp unto my feet. You are near to the faint in spirit. I trust in You and am listening now to Your direction.

11

EASTER

*In his great mercy he has given us new birth into a living hope through
the resurrection of Jesus Christ from the dead, and into an inheritance
that can never perish, spoil or fade—kept in heaven for you.*

1 Peter 1:3–4

Oblivious to our tragedy, the beauty of spring awakened systematically
with its rhythmic cycle. Fresh sweet air flowed through our open
windows and many cheerful dandelions emerged happily about
the lawn, confidently unaware that they were weeds. The earth was
unfolding in miracle and promise, but I was unchanged and stuck in
a nightmare I couldn't force myself to awaken from.

Easter was coming and I will confess, I never cared for Easter
as a child. I should have but did not enjoy the fragrant Easter lilies
with their strange, too-sweet, once-a-year smells. Nor did I like the
loud street preachers who carried crude homemade wooden crosses
through the streets of our community. The showy new clothes, the
fancy hats, and the brand-new shoes of the church congregation
made the center aisle of the sanctuary resemble a fashion runway and

confused my juvenile belief that God's house was a place for humility and simplicity.

Aside from all that, I was especially uncomfortable with the pastor's details about the poor treatment Jesus received during His trial—the beatings and floggings as well as the gory, cruel details surrounding the Crucifixion. I hated the talk of people spitting on Jesus and breaking His legs. I hated the description of a sword piercing His side and nails going through His body. It seemed that some of the teachers of my childhood felt that Christ's sacrifice of bearing our sins on Calvary's cross would be deeply appreciated only in direct proportion to the description of His pain, as if we couldn't value the sacrifice without completely hearing its details. Perhaps there is some merit to that thought, for a cheap sacrifice that cost our dear Lord nothing might surely not be valued as deeply as a death of suffering that cost Him profound spiritual and physical pain.

As a shocked child stuck on the discomfort and horror of the Crucifixion, I must have missed the most significant message of Easter morning, which is the miracle of Christ's resurrection. I must have missed the pastor's glorious description of the miracle of the stone being rolled away, the glory of the angels that announced the good news, and the splendor of Jesus' white-robed appearance. Blinded by the death, my small mind missed the joy of revival.

Easter was different this year, now that my own child had passed from life to death and I was beginning to understand the glorious miracle of the day in a brand-new way. The miraculous resurrection of Jesus Christ from the dead is what gives all believers a tremendous hope that we, too, will rise to dwell in heaven with God. I will see Zachary again simply because of Easter morning. This tremendous measure of hope that promises I will see my son again is bound directly to the power of our Father who snapped the chains of death and broke the bondage of the grave. Because of this work, neither my son, nor I, nor any of those who accept Christ will remain dead, regardless of the manner of our deaths.

In my youth, I had been so captivated by the sadness of death that the joy of the resurrection was lost on me. Now I could feel myself slipping into that pattern again when I thought about Zachary's death. I refused to allow myself that mistake again. While there was much about Zachary's death that I neither liked nor understood, I would fully trust in the hope that he would not stay dead. I would see my son again.

On this first Easter without Zachary, the young children in our family again enjoyed familiar traditions of hunting for plastic Easter eggs, eating jelly beans, and dunking eggs in colorful dyes. We talked about baby chicks and little bunnies and thanked God for the playfulness of all new life during this time of spring's glad renewal. But above all else, we talked about Jesus and His great love for us. We talked about His painful sacrificial death and His glorious resurrection that not only provides the promise of eternal life in heaven for all believers but gives our family the personal hope that we will see our beloved Zachary again.

Dear God,

Zachary is in Your presence now, for his tender heart was devoted to You. You were crucified for my salvation and arose with victory over the grave. Thank You for that gift of eternal life and for the promise of an eternity in heaven.

1 2

OBSESSED
WITH WHY

Because of the L*ord*'s *great love we are not consumed,*
for his compassions never fail.
They are new every morning;
great is your faithfulness.

Lamentations 3:22–23

Hungry for information on the topic of suicide, I searched for information on the Internet, devouring every pamphlet and book that was quietly slipped into my hand or found on the shelves of the public library. Eager to understand the suicidal mind and find the precise explanation for my son's death, I read about mental illness, chemical disturbances, and clinical depression.

Everyone on earth gets depressed now and then from normal life experiences such as financial problems, crumbling relationships, troubles at work, or struggles in school. Most people wrestle with conflict but then rise out of their depression with a resolve to fix whatever was bothering them. For reasons not completely understood, others get stuck and become mired in depression and suicidal thinking. These symptoms include, but are not limited to, persistent sadness, apathy, irritation, and fatigue. Persistent depression may result in appetite and sleep changes, social withdrawal, feelings of worthlessness, and serious thoughts or threats of suicide. Christians who face depression may struggle even more with guilt, because they wonder why they can't seem to "get happy" or access the joy they believe should come from knowing Christ.

To depressed individuals, life is a burden. It is empty and devoid of meaning or purpose. Nothing brings joy or pleasure, and there is no hope for the future. Convinced that no one would ever be able to help, the only desire is for escape from the dreary darkness that fills every waking moment. Individuals choosing suicide make a permanent decision based on insufficient information. In their confused and distorted minds, option A is to continue life as they see it, while option B is to kill themselves and end their pain. Unafraid of dying and more terrified of living, they can't see any other options besides A or B. With struggles too heavy to bear for one moment longer and totally undistracted by the world around them, their distorted judgment musters a fatal decision. Personal pain and suffering are violently ended. They thought the only way to end the pain was by killing it.

I learned that 39,518 Americans took their lives in 2011, which means someone died by suicide every thirteen minutes. Firearms accounted for half of all suicide deaths, and males were four times more likely to choose suicide than females.[1]

From the financially privileged to the struggling lower class, suicide does not discriminate by race, religion, education, IQ, age, or gender. Two-thirds never leave a note[2] and alcohol is suspected to be involved in half of all suicides.[3]

Suicide is the third leading cause of death for youth between the ages of ten and twenty-four, and results in approximately 4,600 losses each year. Within that same age range, 81 percent of the deaths were males and 19 percent were females.[4] A child's suicide is heartbreaking. Most teenagers feel their emotions very deeply and are struggling to find their place in this world. On top of that, some feel misunderstood, out of place, are obsessed with their flaws, or are being bullied. Children naturally have not had enough experience to understand that many of the disappointments in their lives are not life-shattering, but actually rather ordinary. Living only in the moment, they seem incapable of realizing that soon enough there will be another girlfriend, more plays to try out for, another sport to excel in, and additional colleges to apply for. Thousands of kids in communities everywhere endure these types of setbacks every day. Why do some endure these obstacles resiliently while others judge them to be "the end of the world"? Regardless, children should be learning to live, not conspiring to die.

Truly the rain falls on the just and the unjust, for throughout history, and even today, Christian families everywhere have suffered from the poor choices that their loved ones have made. Since recent Gallup polls suggest that 77 percent of the U.S. population claim to be Christians, we can assume that the majority of suicide losses are occurring within homes of people who claim to be believers.[5] Satan's campaign is to destroy Christian families. One way he does this is by working diligently to enhance stigma about suicide and, in doing so, he labors to persuade the world that these types of death do not, and should not, occur within Christian homes. He does this for two

reasons: First, Satan aims to propagate gossip, blame, and scandal
within the Christian community when a suicide does occur. Second,
Satan intends to keep suffering Christian families in bondage to
overwhelming guilt and shame because they have been taught, and it
is often assumed, that suicide shouldn't be happening in their homes.
Satan is not only fervently attacking Christian families whose loved
ones choose suicide but also deceiving the local church who should
be best equipped at ministering to their pain.

My limited understanding of suicide grew alongside my collection
of books, but in spite of all the research and all the professionals in
the world, my arrival at the last page in each volume did not provide
the specific reasons for my own child's death. I was left circling the
event, round and round, examining the experience like a frantic pilot
looking for a safe and final place to land.

I spent every waking moment trying to pinpoint what had
been the cause of Zachary's hopelessness and despairing choice that
a violent death would be easier than continuing his life. The *why*
glared at me when I awoke, followed me much too closely all day
long, preying upon me and taunting me like a fearsome animal I
couldn't slay. It grabbed me by the collar of my shirt and shook me
in interrogation, insisting that I scrutinize every past event I could
remember, demanding that I answer every repeated question until
satisfactory evidence could be provided. The *why* lingered coldly
within me in the nighttime long after I turned out the lights and
waited there restlessly, poised and ready to pounce at any moment to
wake me for another torturous round.

My life was nothing but an obsession of his death. Drawn to
what I could not understand and obsessed with the unknown, I
became Nancy Drew with an ever-present magnifying glass searching

as a detective would for clues. Although I knew the perpetrator and the victim, the how and the where, I could not solve the why of this murder mystery. Completely baffled, I returned to Zachary's things again and again, examining his school papers and searching his wallet, rechecking the pockets of his jackets, and analyzing his drawings. My sleuthing resulted in no substance and even less speculation, for I found no clues or any motive for Zachary's suicide. Even the toxicology report from his autopsy showed no alcohol or drug abuse. Was there nothing to explain why a kind sixteen-year-old boy would kill himself?

Maybe the police investigators needed to come back. Maybe I needed some kind of a trained professional to analyze this horrible event and type a summary neatly for me to read. Someone please tell me exactly what happened so that I don't kill another of my children with my carelessness or negligence or selfishness. I promise I will do better. I promise I won't let it happen again.

I was on a miserable, dizzy ride on a merry-go-round, an unrelenting journey of monotonous torturing questions. Securely fastened on a horse I couldn't get off, around and around I went as the pit of my stomach complained and begged for relief. With crazy carnival music blaring in my head, I jerked up and down, spinning faster and faster. There was no release, no escape, and no mechanism to stop this crazed experience. "The truth will set you free" took on new meaning. If I didn't have the truth, would I always be in bondage to his death?

Although I was obsessed with finding a reason, I had to admit that maybe a reason wouldn't even have made sense. And it definitely wouldn't have brought my son back. Perhaps I would somehow have to learn to live with unanswered questions for the rest of my life.

Perhaps the *why* would one day quiet down and shrink back into the shadows. I would wait and see, knowing fully that if God chose not to supply me with the solutions to my many confusing questions, then He surely instead would provide me with grace to live without the answers.

Dear God,

This unfamiliar road is without signposts and I am not a skilled traveler, yet perhaps, if I try, I can follow You courageously without needing to know exactly where You are taking me. You will lead me safely home.

1 3

GUILTY

The Spirit helps us in our weakness. We do not know what
we ought to pray for, but the Spirit himself intercedes
for us with groans that words cannot express.

Romans 8:26

Mother's Day bloomed on a gorgeous day in May, and although it served as a painful reminder that I had lost a child, it was also a cause for celebration. Recently the parental rights of the two siblings we had been fostering for over a year had been terminated and we signed adoption papers to make these children permanent members of our family. Allen and I felt exceedingly blessed and chose to take a temporary break from fostering more children.

Like Hannah of old, motherhood was a high calling, a great privilege, and a profound honor. Caring for children was a passion deeply embedded in my heart. It defined who I was.

In pregnancy, it is the mother's necessary heartbeat and rhythmic blood flow of her own life force that fundamentally keeps her child alive. While I was pregnant, my very breath sustained Zachary's unborn life and after he was delivered, maybe I never let go of the notion that I was fully capable of sustaining the two of us.

With the birth of each of my children, I felt an overwhelming responsibility for every little one's well-being. I welcomed each infant with a humble and sincere vow to be a good parent, and that driving force motivated everything I chose all day long. With a fierce desire to protect and keep them safe, many were the times I cradled my children safely in my arms, pledging to take care of them, promising that they would never be alone. Many were the times my fervent prayers took over when inexperience and lofty dreams failed.

Repeatedly I asked God for deep and specific insight into each child's personality, imploring Him to grant me understanding of how each child ticked. Like a metal detector programmed to pick up subtle clues about what is under the ground, I was vigilant and sensitive as I prayerfully tried to decode the personalities and needs of each child.

I took mothering literally and felt responsible for every discomfort of my child. If he was cold because his diaper was wet or agitated because his belly was hungry, I was responsible. When he tripped because his shoes were too big or fell in the mud because I wasn't holding his hand, I figured it was my fault for slacking off.

Likewise, my child's every success boosted my self-esteem and reflected positively on me as a mother. His clean button-downed shirt, fresh haircut, and courteous manners conveyed the message that an attentive parent was involved. When he recited his Bible verses and received good math scores, I assumed I was on the right track.

Now the myth of good parenting taunted and sneered at me. Hadn't I been taught to believe that excellent parenting produced great kids and to assume that lousy parenting amounted to wayward

children? Now I had flunked motherhood. I had received a big, fat
F on my report card. I had failed to keep Zachary alive, and this
accusation chanted in my head.

Ever since our children were infants, safety was a huge issue.
We used outlet covers, cabinet locks, bunk bed rails, and two coats
of sunscreen. The children heard many repetitive reminders: "Put
on your seat belt!" "Wear a bike helmet!" "Don't climb too high
in that tree." We admonished them not to talk to strangers, never
swim alone, to lock the front door, and to wear hearing protection
when they'd mow, goggles when they'd drill, and elbow pads when
they'd rollerblade. We had fully taught the children to care for and
safeguard their lives. I had to realize that despite my best intentions,
I had failed to anticipate and shield my child from every danger.

Sixteen years ago, God had entrusted a little boy into my care
for safekeeping and that child had died on my watch. Like a formal
soldier guarding the castle with proper protocol, I had been a sentinel
on duty. Given a momentous responsibility, I had failed and the
negligence stared me in the face. I also questioned my role as a foster
parent, consumed with the idea that while I had been trying to save
other people's children, I had lost one of my own. I questioned my
choice to have a large family, fixated on the notion that I hadn't done
enough to keep one child from slipping through the cracks.

As a mother, vigilance and love were the two essential parenting
techniques I had relied on to sustain my child. Now they both had
sorely failed and bitterly betrayed me. I had poured my life into my
child and found there to be a cruel hole in the bottom of the bucket.
I had not succeeded despite my best attempts at good parenting,
common sense, and unconditional devotion. My compass was badly
broken and I was without direction, as lost as a traveler with no map

and no guideposts. Perhaps I wanted to throw in the child-raising towel. After all, how on earth could I trust in my abilities to bring up my remaining children?

I felt Zachary had not only rejected his own life but the life we had created for him. As parents, we had selected his school curriculum, chosen his church, and assigned his chores. We had bought his vegetables, planned his vacations, and purchased his clothes. Parenting with a godly Christian hedge of protection against evil, we had set boundaries about music and movies, friends and entertainment. Zachary sat in the middle of all of that living, powerless and submissive, completely under the rule and guidance of someone other than himself. If he was unhappy with his life, wasn't that the result of his parents who had created so much of what he knew to be his life? His death felt to be a blatant accusation that things weren't what he wanted or, more important, what he needed. Guilt gnawed at my heart.

I wanted to be free from the bondage of this emotional jail cell I was confined to. I decided one day to sit down and make a list, starting with a title across the top of the page: Things I Did Right. I wrote down every good thing I had ever provided for Zachary: food, clothes, love, laughter, apologies, birthdays, vacations. I wrote and wrote, feeling the words come confidently and quickly, and noticed that the chains of guilt were loosening around my heart as quickly as my pen flew. The list got longer and longer, proving that I had responsibly raised this child—as I did all my children—with love, intent, and creativity.

The whole time Zachary was growing up, I never had a bad intention or a malicious motive to hurt or hinder him in any way. To the contrary, we had placed boundaries around him out of love to protect his heart, his character, and his very life. We had hoped that any guideline he thought was unfair or unreasonable had paled in comparison to the many freedoms and enriching experiences we had brought into his life.

No, I wasn't a perfect mother. I was crabby when I had a headache and stressed when the day got hectic. I was impatient over spilled milk and frustrated from the constant bickering on rainy afternoons. Every parent can look back and see times when they wish they had done better, for regardless of a parent's love, it is impossible to raise a child without mistakes. God has not called us to model perfection, but only to demonstrate our best and most genuine imperfect love within the boundaries of our God-created personalities.

Setting aside my tendencies toward guilt, I resolved to stop berating myself for not being perfect and instead gave myself permission to have been the best parent I knew how to be. I purposed to make peace with my shortcomings and to fully accept my failures and inadequacies. Sifting through the past, I pledged to take ownership of only what I was solely responsible for. Any offenses that I brought against Zachary shouldn't have resulted in his choice to end his life. Surely his rationale for dying exceeded my parenting mishaps, and he let his reasons be reasons enough.

Dear God,

I poured great efforts into being a successful parent but did not always model godliness before the watchful eyes of my children. Please forgive me for the sins of my past and release me from the powerful gripping chains of this guilt.

1 4

DEPRESSED

You have made known to me the path of life;
you will fill me with joy in your presence,
with eternal pleasures at your right hand.

Psalm 16:11

The summer went by with blazing heat. My flowers shriveled and died because I did not water them, and the garden vegetables choked with weeds because I did not tend them. I was parched and constantly thirsty but found no oasis in the desert. Everything about me felt severely and painfully blistered, as if I had an emotional sunburn that produced constant agony.

Sadness had taken up permanent residence in every portion of my being. Life was nothing short of an obligation, and the future held no promise of joy. I felt that someone had brought in a very large injection needle to anesthetize me, for I was emotionally disabled and completely inoculated against pleasure. I barely existed in a dense fog of shock and pain as the days went by numbly one by one, each as unchanging as the day before.

My entire life was on hold. The clock meant nothing; time stood still. I spent many hours on the couch with a quilt thrown over my body, pitifully licking my wounds. I clung to the grief and wrapped it around myself, afraid that if I ever were to stop thinking of Zachary, the memories would fade and I would truly be left with nothing of my son.

Hour by hour, the mantra was simple: "Breathe in. Breathe out." I listened to my heart, felt every different emotion that came, and tried to accept each one as a part of the grieving process. Out of necessity, I was fully self-centered and completely unapologetic about it. I was in a canyon hearing the voices of others echo off the steep walls, oblivious to what was going on around me while also fully aware that I was missing out on life.

I felt empty, useless, and barely able to give my children the love and attention they needed. The laughter and joy were gone from my life, and I wondered what kind of a mother had been exchanged for the one they knew. Mechanically performing each task on autopilot, I drove the kids to birthday parties, stirred the chili for dinner, put gas in the car, and purchased groceries. Did any of these chores matter? Would anything in my life ever matter again? I no longer knew.

Zachary's death was a true amputation with no anesthesia, no bandages, and no pain medication. I was truly crippled. The pain was unbearable, and I felt I needed morphine. When my friends asked me how I was doing, I felt like saying, "If I told you, I would scare you." This task asked more of me than I had to give, taking far more effort than I could muster. I was exhausted and drained of resources.

I tried, but I could not live without Zachary. As I slipped to low and dark places I never knew existed, suffering and depression became a predictable void. I was frightened by the intensity of despair in my own mind but hadn't a clue what to do. I barely wanted to live. I constantly made mental lists of why life was difficult and repeatedly doubted the value of living. Wouldn't death bring me freedom from this pain? Wouldn't it bring me to Zachary? The consuming desire for relief was hard to ignore.

Satan had successfully lured one family member away and was working overtime on me now, for I was his next project. Constantly he announced each personal shortcoming and barked accusing lists of my failures and inadequacies. In my weakest moments, hearing his condemning voice in my ear made me wonder if there could be anything good about my life, if there could be anything good about me.

Fighting the deep depression that constantly hovered over each day proved for many months to be the toughest battle of my life. As I focused on my family and begged God for strength, staying alive became my number-one priority. Each day's limited amount of energy was spent on the war against hopelessness. Although I didn't know Zachary's specific desperation, I tasted my own and could now fully imagine how the nagging despair had driven him to his death. My own suffering helped me glimpse his pain and empathize with his misery.

I wondered what Zachary would think to see me now? He would be devastated to find out that his death had wounded me so deeply that I could barely manage my life's responsibilities. He would be shocked to see me in this slimy pit and would long for my happiness and healing, just as I longed for his.

On that fateful day that Zachary took his own life, if I would have arrived home just a few hours earlier and found him still alive with that gun in his hands, what would I have said to him? What speech would I have earnestly delivered? Would I have reminded Zachary that this life is called a race because it requires a huge amount of endurance? Would I have reminded him that trials and troubles fade but perseverance brings an eternal reward? Would I have told him that God would never forsake him, but instead would provide just enough strength and grace for each day? Whatever speech I would have given to my child was the very speech I now needed to give to myself. Whatever I would have done to save my own child's life, I now needed to do for myself.

As much as I wanted the relief of dying, I wanted even more to live. I had two choices, just like Zachary, for before me God had set life and death, and I clearly knew which path He required of me. Whatever my quality of life was and however it would continue to be, I knew I wanted to live, fully confident that this choice was far better, for me and for my family, than the alternative.

If I were to live, then God would have to teach me how, and I begged Him for this help with many prayers that began with the best of intentions but often faded into incomplete sentences. I barely knew how to pray and frequently didn't even have the strength to try, but God didn't need my words. He met me in my suffering and fully understood my heart. Faithful both in the past and during this crisis, He was never out of reach or earshot.

Zachary had lost his battle for life, and I would now win it in his honor. It did not matter how slow I plodded and stumbled, as long as I kept plodding and stumbling, clinging to the age-old technique of putting one foot in front of the other. With God's help, I would prove it could be done.

Dear God,

You are near the brokenhearted. Please infuse Your life into mine by breathing the power of Your love into my own lungs. I wait patiently for renewal, as You supply me with all things, and only those essentials, that are necessary for life.

1 5

ANGRY

Turn your ear to me,
come quickly to my rescue.

Psalm 31:2

Many wild, predictable summer thunderstorms moved in quickly with their drenching noise, interfering with playful neighborhood activities and sending children running for the safety of their homes. In the same way, the torrential floods of grief often interrupted my routine with their chaos, canceled whatever composure I might have been calmly preserving, and forced me to address whatever immediate emotion lay in front of me.

Zachary was gone because of a senseless and violent death—he had purposefully destroyed himself. Anger began to rear its ugly head.

I had interrupted my life every two hours to nourish his infant body, had stayed up at night to soothe him when he was ill, and had rocked away every crying fit with patience and patting. I had willingly spent money and lost sleep, exerted energy and forfeited spontaneity. I had nurtured and valued him for more than sixteen years. All out of love. For what? I did not raise him for this.

I was resentful toward Zachary for leaving Allen and me. I was angry that we had been forced to perform emotional CPR on his brothers and sisters and required to watch the suffering of his grandparents, aunts, uncles, and cousins. What had happened to the bond we had shared, the relationships we had enjoyed, the things we had taken pleasure doing together? Didn't he value that attachment, that friendship? What right did one person have to violently ruin the lives of so many others? How could one person cause so much suffering and control me now just because he had been so out of control himself? Rendered powerless and totally at the mercy of his actions, I was required to get a broom and dustpan to clean up this mess. I was enraged!

Zachary had voluntarily exited his life without an explanation. Obviously there had been a problem, but Zachary had been unwilling to talk or listen. All dialogue ended. Discussion over. Case closed. I was now sitting across the table from an empty chair, left with only an unfinished conversation. The door had been slammed in my face, and I wanted to beat my fists on it. For the rest of my days, I would have to question the depth of my own involvement. I would forever be hiking up my self-esteem just as one tugs on a pair of large, ill-fitting pants.

Had I wasted my time with homeschooling, with Sunday school, with youth activities? Had it been in vain that we allowed only G-rated movies or the local PBS station? What was the point of having a safety password for the Internet on the home computer? I had tried so hard to protect my children from the evils of the world. How could it be that I obviously hadn't even been able to protect my son from himself?

I was furious with Satan. He knows exactly how to stalk and harass each of us in our most vulnerable moments of weakness. Keen for opportunity, he grabs on to the fears and insecurities of those who are troubled or emotionally frail and attempts to persuade them of the value of ending their pain by killing it. Satan introduced Zachary to death with a convincing offer of escape and reprieve. As if following a flashing neon sign welcoming all weary travelers, my child was enticed to enter the world of dying. Death became his new friend, his only friend, his last friend.

Mostly I was angry with myself. How could I have not noticed Zachary's distress? Every day he walked up and down our stairs, in and out of our kitchen. Had I never even perceived that his life was in trouble? How could I have been so blind and inattentive? I would never forgive myself!

I would never have the pleasure of watching Zachary grow into adulthood, have a career, perhaps get married and raise children. I would never know if he would have found something in this life to be passionate about or someone in this world to deeply love. I wanted to yell at his photo and tell him how in one single moment he had stolen my dreams and robbed the future. I felt punished, penalized. He had put himself into his own grave. I was angry that we owned a cemetery plot and could now only be near his body by visiting it.

My entire reputation was ruined. Were people studying and dissecting our every parenting interaction with the other children for possible signs to explain Zachary's death? My peaceful country home had been violated by his death. Did people in the community slow down when they drove past? Did they point, look at each other in horror, and whisper, "That's where it happened?" I did not deserve this!

There was now a dangerous cavern in my heart where my son used to be. It was marked with orange construction cones and roped off with yellow plastic caution tape. I was required to tiptoe with hesitation lest I get sucked into a disastrous mishap and lose my composure, mindful that any loose stones or soft dirt would send me slipping quickly down its treacherous steep slopes.

We had inherited a new haunting family legacy and would have to tell the next generation about this person in the scrapbook who was dead by suicide. It was an inheritance bequeathed to me that I did not choose and was not in any way proud of. I would forever be skirting difficult topics, dancing around tricky subject matter, and forced into the embarrassing task of answering awkward and complicated questions concerning my family size.

In August, a recent birthday card had read, "Wishing you all the things that make you the happiest." Happiest? I would never reach "happiest" again. I might be happy and happier, but only having my whole precious family intact would make me happiest. The joy of my birthday, like all of the joys to come in my life, had been brought down a notch, like a radio that won't play the highest volume or my broken kitchen mixer that cannot spin on the highest speed. There were now a few coffee grounds and a bitter taste at the bottom of every cup we lifted.

Once while I towel dried the kitchen plates, I surprised myself by wondering how they would sound if they were flung crashing through the glass windows.

I was livid at the way my life had turned out.

Dear God,

Please silence my turmoil and sweep this fury from my mind. Do not harden my heart, for I don't want to become cynical and bitter. Help me to examine the deep secret places of my being, so that I may confess each sin and live free of shame.

1 6

I AM ACQUITTED

Test me, O Lord, and try me,
examine my heart and my mind;
for your love is ever before me,
and I walk continually in your truth.

Psalm 26:2–3

Somewhere in my life I had learned that it was not only wrong to insult God by questioning Him, but it was particularly sinful to be annoyed or angry about troubling events that unfolded around me. As a child, submission and humility had been stressed, as well as full respect for God's sovereignty.

Yet for me, a valid relationship with God had to be based on honesty. Nothing less would be satisfactory. This tragedy had deepened my faith and created a very intimate spiritual friendship that was based on transparency. I was not afraid to tell God exactly how I felt, for as His child, I had full confidence that I would neither offend nor anger my Father.

Zachary's suicide had given me valid reason to be confused and angry. I had cause to stomp my feet and holler. God knew that, and

He was totally capable of handling all of my most foolish temper tantrums. Nothing could separate me from Him, and because I felt deeply known and intimately understood, I clung to Him even more because of this valid acceptance.

And so the anger sometimes roared like a fire-breathing dragon. But after I had finished stomping my feet like a raging two-year-old and had thoroughly exhausted myself with each fuming outburst, the anger burned itself out. Like an untied balloon slipping out of someone's hand, the fury deflated quickly, leaving me only flat and empty.

How could I be angry? My unconditional love for Zachary glowed eternally. I accepted all of his human quirks and sins with a mother's devoted affection. I loved him completely and defensively. How could I stay angry at someone who had been so full of despair and hopelessness that he acted violently against himself? How could I stay angry at someone who felt so miserable and unhappy that he had taken his own life, settling for far less than what was meant to be?

I had to believe that Zachary was lost—deeply lost in a thick maze, a blinding snowstorm, or a hazy fog. He was wandering in a barren desert, caught in a confusing tunnel, and he craved rescue, not death. I couldn't quite believe Zachary wanted to quit. I think he had no clue how to continue.

It broke my heart to consider the dark place my son must have been in as he battled an internal enemy and tried to conquer the depression that was draining his strength, his courage, and his very life. A wounded warrior, he became a casualty of his own war, and died on his own battlefield. I grieve for him in his desperate search for peace.

God is a father, the most perfect of fathers. Have all of His children throughout the ages followed His teaching, heeded His advice, and made their own good choices based on His wise instruction? Of course not! If God is not being held accountable for the poor choices of His children, neither am I to be blamed for the dire choices of mine. God let Zachary's free will determine his future. God's kingdom is full of hope, meaning, purpose, and life. Satan's empire is all about despair, chaos, futility, and death. I am not a biblical expert or a theologian, but I do believe that we live in a world of good and evil and that one of God's good gifts to His children is free will. Since the creation of Adam and Eve, man has been exercising that gift and reaping the consequences of it.

Although Allen and I purposefully tried to teach our children godly values and basic morality, we also had taught them since they were tiny that they made their own choices and were responsible for their own actions. Didn't this principle still apply, even in the face of a suicide death? Why did I feel as if my son should not be held accountable for walking into the woods that day to end his life? I should not be held responsible for a decision I did not make. Was I so disillusioned with the memory of my child's greatness that it felt cruel to blame him for such a death? Did it feel kinder to place fault on my own shoulders rather than to heap it onto the shoulders of a wounded child?

Zachary was sixteen years old and knew right from wrong. He had not consulted me, asked for my authorization, or sought my approval. I had not condoned this idea or signed my name on some field trip permission slip. He was gone now in this horrible way—his way. He had never asked me for help to whatever problem he was facing or demanded that something change in his life. He hadn't given a hint, dropped a clue, or made any threat that would cause us to take immediate action and offer direction. Zachary hadn't given us a chance to understand his pain but had faced his giants on his own terms, in his own silence, with his own free will. If something I had done or failed to do was causing him such misery, shouldn't he have told me? If I never knew he had a need, how could I be held accountable for not meeting it?

Very slowly over time, I began to believe that Zachary was responsible for his own death. Suicide was not a rational choice, nor a sensible choice, but it was Zachary's choice. However hopeless and confused he felt, he had chosen this fate. I could not own this death. I was innocent.

That was the final verdict.

Dear God,

My prison doors unlock with Your forgiveness. I deeply regret Zachary's poor choice, but I am not responsible for it. Please forgive all who die by their own hands, for they do not fully know what they do to themselves or to those of us left behind.

1 7

LONELY

By his light I walked through darkness!

Job 29:3

How could the world continue on its normal course when mine had so abruptly stopped? How could people carry their shopping bags out of stores, stand in line at the bank, or eat in fine restaurants when my child was dead? Why wasn't the world pausing with me to deal with this tragedy? I wanted to raise a flag at half-mast in front of my home, forever flapping in the breeze to announce this tragedy. I wanted to yell and scream to the whole world, "Something happened to me! Something happened that completely changed my life, and I will never be the same! My life has stopped! My child is DEAD!"

I was a new person and felt it was now impossible for anyone to understand who I had become. I knew no one personally outside of my family who had lived through a loved one's suicide and because of this isolation, grieving Zachary's death became a very lonely and solitary existence. Known now as "the mom whose kid killed himself," I didn't want people to raise their eyebrows, avert their eyes, or quickly turn to walk in the other direction. I didn't want to be judged or criticized, pitied or shunned. Were some people afraid of me? Was I a reminder that if a suicide death could happen to our family, then it could possibly happen to theirs?

Some smiled and talked about mundane things like the unusual weather or the rising price of gas. How could they chatter through such small talk when I stood before them practically bleeding to death? Were they afraid to mention Zachary's name? Did they need to tiptoe around our family's eggshells? Perhaps it seemed safer for people to say nothing at all about our tragedy rather than risk adding to our grief with what they feared might be an inappropriate conversation.

I quietly moved to the perimeters of some small-talk circles, because I had little tolerance for listening to moms whine and gripe about their kids and the ball games they had to transport them to, or the new school shoes they had to buy, or the fresh mud all over the clean kitchen floor. I couldn't deal with complaints about large grocery bills and bikes left out in the rain. I tried to listen politely, but comments like these from tired and stressed moms only made my heart ache. I wanted to yell, "Just be glad your kid is alive enough to create dirty laundry, alive enough to forget to feed the cat, alive enough to leave their rollerblades where people will trip over them!"

I backed quietly into my own shell. My perspective had changed because of death. I was a refurbished and reconditioned mom. Parenting was indeed the toughest job around, but it was an immense blessing. For those of us who wished our child were still alive to provide us with that tough job, it was a blessing we would no longer enjoy.

There were some people who seemed to think I had spent enough time grieving Zachary's death. They insisted I needed "to move on," "get over it," or "focus on something else." I guess since they had easily returned to their own lives, I was expected to return to mine. Tired of my tears and weary of my grief, some tugged at my arm, trying to hurry me through my pain. But I was not a child with a skinned knee who could be distracted with a lollipop.

Others were bold enough to chastise me for my gloom. "You need more faith!" or "Aren't you over this yet?" Those comments only added to my isolation and sadness. Was I doing something wrong? Should these who had never walked in my boots be telling me to pull myself up by my bootstraps?

I was too weary to say much. I would mourn alone if others tired of me. I would distance myself or steer clear from those who wanted to determine what my timetable for grief ought to be. Zachary's death was not just a bump in the road to swerve around or a fallen tree to climb over. I wished people understood that I was no longer even on the same road and was totally clueless about where this unfamiliar drive was taking me.

A few individuals simply could not deal with any aspect of Zachary's suicide or our devastation by it. I tried not to perceive their instinctive discomfort as rejection, but truth be told, I watched some friendships pause because of fear and misinformation, while other relationships dissolved from judgmental attitudes and lack of compassion.

As disappointed as I was by those who could not understand the significance of my loss or the intensity of my pain, I was even more blessed by those who did. These brave friends and family members continued to bring their own sons and daughters to my house to play with my children and were courageous enough to say the word "suicide" out loud. They came straight up to me, looked into my eyes, and with no intent to pry, asked the hard and messy questions about Zachary's death. They never flinched at my words, never turned away in disgust, never wearily checked their watches for the time or excused themselves to complete some necessary errand.

These wise ones, somewhere along the way, had learned that the greatest gift they could give is an offer to listen. Their tender gift blotted my wounds. I needed to talk about Zachary and I did, saying the same things again and again as I heard his name roll off my tongue. Peeling back the layers of the onion, telling Zachary's story was my strongest need and the only way that I could figure out what his death meant to me.

Forever I am thankful for these dear ones who set aside their own fears and were open-minded enough to become educated about suicide. Tearing down walls of stigma and shame, they helped take away some of the isolation and blame that was crushing me. During this dark season of my life, I was far too crippled with grief and much too consumed with selfishness to be a good friend, yet I was grateful to all who waited patiently for me to crawl out of my darkness. Without growing weary or feeling overburdened, these valiant friends continued to reach out to me even when they received so little in return. My healing was largely due to their understanding and patience, and I am forever appreciative of their gentle love.

Dear God,

You were no stranger to loneliness. Despite the solitude of this valley, I have never been alone. You answer every time I call and never turn a deaf ear to my requests. Please satisfy every longing with the promises of Your Word.

1 8

THE BEACH

Blessed is he ...
*whose hope is in the L*ORD *his God,*
the Maker of heaven and earth,
the sea, and everything in them—
*the L*ORD*, who remains faithful forever.*

Psalm 146:5–6

In September, six months after Zachary's death, someone kindly offered us the weekend use of a beach house, and we jumped at the golden opportunity. It had been years since our family had vacationed at the beach and the thought of experiencing something different, something other than an unchanging pattern of grief, seemed a refreshing and welcome idea.

The children were excited. Some had never been to the seashore and eagerly packed bathing suits, suntan lotion, and plastic buckets with grand hopes of building castles and collecting seashells. The long car trip hardly deterred their enthusiasm for the adventure ahead.

They were not to be disappointed, for without the intense heat of summer, the delightful days that followed were peaceful and unique. Here in a beautiful beach house there were no keepsakes of Zachary, no rooms filled with family photographs, and nothing to tease us with reminders of how life used to be. There was just our family together in simplicity and the beautiful shoreline before us outstretching an enticing offer to set aside our grief and try something new in this sandy sanctuary.

Daily, the children played in the sand for hours and delighted in this surprising playground at their fingertips. They dug holes and made pies, running back to the ocean for water again and again, and all the while fully focused on the magic before them. They skipped delightedly along the shore collecting buckets of mostly broken shells, and I marveled at the fact that, like God our Father, these little ones found beauty in things that were imperfect or utterly flawed.

I wondered about these damaged shells that once had been beautifully intact. Where had they come from? What life had they known? Surely the foamy turbulent waves and coastal storms had moved them far from the places they knew, and with discomfort and confusion had landed them on a distant foreign shore. It humored me to feel a connection with wet chipped shells, and while I pondered the mysteries behind their arrival, I watched them serve a new purpose of bringing delight, regardless of their flaws, to the ones with eyes to appreciate their beauty.

Allen and I did little more than lounge in our beach chairs, relish the pleasant breezes, and enjoy the children's happiness. Sitting there with the native grasses swaying on the sand dunes behind me, there was something mesmerizing about hearing the gentle waves lap in their rhythmic musical cadence while young happy voices laughed and called to each other. Something deep within me was soothed, and I felt a wellspring of hope to know that my children could find pleasure and peace in this lovely place.

The long walks on the beach were calming. I found it refreshing to breathe in the salty air with all its smells of marine life and sea creatures while I searched for sea glass or smooth rocks that had bounced about on the abrasive ocean floor. The immense open water and wide beckoning sky challenged the parts of my heart that had been getting smaller and tighter during the past six months. It was revitalizing to watch the soaring seagulls squawk shrilly and swoop wildly for their meals while delicate sandpipers hurried about nervously leaving tiny footprints on the damp white sand. My senses, previously seized up stiffly in the routine of grief, now unlocked and eagerly worked overtime to welcome each sea life sensation. With fresh surprise, I marveled at the wonders before me.

My heartache over Zachary's choice had followed me to this vacation wonderland, and I noticed how much my grief was like the tides of this sea, ebbing and flowing, pushing and pulling. Never quite certain of when an unexpected wave would knock me to my feet, I could rise choking and sputtering to regain my balance, rein in my composure, and promise myself to not be caught off guard again.

When the children tired of the beach, we took leisurely walks to the park or caught the drips from melting ice cream cones at the neighborhood parlor. In this small beach town, the locals were good-natured and knew nothing of our story. Their faces were friendly, with eyes neither full of pity or suspicion, and it felt good to be somewhere where we felt so totally anonymous and appeared completely normal.

When our vacation ended, it was wistful—almost sad—to leave this place of serenity. Mindful that this type of tranquility could not be packed as a souvenir and removed from the beach, we left it behind and took with us instead an appreciation for the restful vacation we had enjoyed. There, where the seagulls and sandpipers would remain, we knew we would return again and again to find among them and their coastal habitat a true rejuvenation of mind, body, and spirit.

Heading back to the peaceful grazing animals and scenic timeworn barns of the farmland environment I was familiar with, we returned to our home, to our life, and to our story with a renewed hope for healing. Having learned the merit of a restful vacation, we made a vow to make this a new family tradition.

We all agreed. We'd be back.

Dear God,

You are magnificently revealed in all of creation, and I turn my eyes reverently upon You with awe. I rejoice to experience all of the marvels of nature and thank You for the refreshing reprieve we have experienced here in this place of peace.

19

CONFIDENT OF
MY BELIEFS

Now I know in part; then I shall know fully, even as I am fully known.

1 Corinthians 13:12

Throughout history, humans have always been at the mercy of their loved ones' choices. Because of this, believers have never been exempt from the suicides of people they love.

Christian families, however strong or full of faith, are sometimes forced to suffer through this confusing tragedy with an extra measure of complication because of conflicting biblical beliefs within the Christian community. Although all of the suicide deaths in the Bible are recorded factually like any other kind of death with no sin judgment attached to their stories, society has created its own stigma and even most Christians who hear of a suicide occurring have strong personal beliefs concerning this type of death.

While most people were definitely uncomfortable about Zachary's suicide, others were confident enough about their opinions to boldly share them with me. I was most offended by those who teach that people who die by suicide have committed an unforgivable sin and could never enter heaven. Was this in the Bible? Those who held this judgmental belief created barriers of discomfort and criticism, and instead of offering compassion, they bluntly gave no hope for my son's soul. With bleak predictions and awkward silences, their alienation made me feel that Zachary had been too naughty for heaven and, like a disruptive student, had been reprimanded and sent to sit out in the hall.

Would one final act at death by a child of God keep someone from enjoying an eternity with their Father? Could one secluded event of confusion now cancel out a lifetime of commitment and loving service to Christ?

God looks upon all He has made with compassionate eyes, not condemning of human frailties. He is best at empathizing with troubled hearts and confused minds. God alone knows what conversations were voiced right before someone's death and what outstanding sins were confessed and which accounts were settled. Only God understands a man's faith commitment and the intent of his mind. God is qualified to fairly look at the complete picture of a person's life.

Some believers were bound and determined to persuade me of their opinion that this suicide death was a part of God's preplanned, sovereign design, and that Zachary's death was orchestrated for the advancement of His divine purpose. I was challenged, as a good Christian, to obediently submit to this work and even be joyful about it, because in some kind of a strategic way, God was mysteriously working out a magnificent outcome in exchange for my son's life.

Scripture definitely seemed confusing to me regarding God's sovereign plan, His power to control the course of events, and His ability to do as He pleases. As I studied these verses, each interpretation measuring God's level of involvement concerning my son's death directly colored the way I saw my heavenly Father.

For every Christian wanting to tell me what I should believe, there was another standing nearby with a different theory. Some Christians were confident that the suicide was Satan's fault and with quickness gave him the complete blame for my family's sorrow. Others referenced the story of Job and believed that after a spiritual tug of war, Satan had been given full permission from God to tempt our son.

I did not want Zachary's death to cause division or be turned into a theological debate. The loss of our son had caused enough suffering and chaos within our family, and I greatly craved peace. The circular discussions some insisted on repeating did nothing but cause me great weariness and stress.

Yes, God permitted Satan to test Job, and I could spend the rest of my life pondering God's role on the day of my son's death and debating whether or not He chose Zachary, and our entire family for that matter, to endure this experience. Did God want Zachary to die that day to carry out some purpose for His heavenly plan? Or was it Satan that was determined to secure Zachary's death for his own evil scheme? Was the suicide divine or demonic?

Amid my confusion, I had my own beliefs. They were fairly simple: God wouldn't ask my child to commit murder, evil exists in this world we dwell in, and each of us has been gifted with a free will. I could not believe that God had orchestrated this suicide, stamped His approval on the event, or ordered an iron-fisted command that required my son to be controlled by puppet strings for the Master's pleasure. Yes, God could absolutely use Zachary's death to advance His purposes, and I sincerely prayed that He would do so with my willing efforts to share my son's story, but the God I knew would never demand the act of self-murder from my child.

While there would always be much concerning my son's death that I would never understand, I have chosen to focus soundly on the concept that God is called I AM, not "I did" or "I didn't." It is far less important for me to know God's role on the day of my son's death and so much more vital that I trust in the faithful attributes of God's loving character that are close to me every day.

As Christians, many of us spend our lives learning to understand God, pursuing that study more earnestly as we age, mature, and process many complicated life experiences. We go to church and study theology, all the while learning principles and techniques to better interpret God's Word. While truly it is biblically profitable to seek God, perhaps the danger would lie in the presumed arrival of complete understanding. For if we ever reached the point where we claimed to fully grasp God on an intellectual level or when we think we have Him all figured out, we might end our search to know Him more deeply. We would cease listening and have no need for the kind of faith that requires us to trust in what we cannot understand.

While I'd like to think that I deeply know God, it is obvious that my personal beliefs have enormous gaps that are filled only with hidden mystery. Embracing these secrets in a dynamic search to know God further is what draws me to a more profound relationship with Him and keeps me coming back for more. Mystery keeps me searching.

Dear God,

Your Word reveals the truth of Your faithful character. Please continue to speak to me as You unveil all the secrets You wish for me to know. I will trust in what I understand and patiently wait to learn the mysteries I cannot grasp.

2 0

HIS BIRTHDAY

*Every good and perfect gift is from above, coming down from the Father
of the heavenly lights, who does not change like shifting shadows.*

James 1:17

Summer wound down and was pushed aside by autumn as the stores
boasted sales on fall apparel and the children excitedly stepped into
a new school year. The local apple orchards were heavily laden with
fruit, and the nervous squirrels with cheeks full of nuts hoarded away
their winter supplies. The crisp fall air failed to bring me delight and
the vivid colors on the trees fell short of providing me with their
usual pleasure. My life was as dull and brittle as the leftover husks in
the harvested autumn fields. Above me the noisy geese were making
their V formation and leaving town, as if in rejection of what they
knew the future here would be. I wanted to join them and escape to
a more promising place.

Zachary's seventeenth birthday was arriving, and with it, the
heartache of deciding what to do on such a special occasion. Nothing
seemed quite right, for this day had always been a reflection of our

son's particular interests on any given year. Throughout Zachary's childhood, we had enjoyed many colorful birthday cakes decorated with trains, airplanes, and race cars. As he got older and his fascinations changed, birthday parties had themes of pirates, cowboys, and favorite movie characters. Always, there had been piles of gifts—some that Zachary requested—and others we were certain he would love.

Now he wasn't here to choose. He wasn't here at all. How could we celebrate a birthday when the guest of honor wasn't present?

Allen and I finally decided to take the children to release helium balloons at Zachary's headstone. While we watched the colorful balloons gently float up into the bright blue sky, my tears of frustration and sadness were carried away with them on the wind. Looking into the heavens and imagining my son there, I whispered a quiet "Happy birthday, Zachary." There was little else to do.

This day had affected each family member differently, but I especially noticed how sad my husband was on this day. Allen lived for Christ in a confident and calm manner and as a heroic warrior, sought to protect his family from the Enemy's many attacks. He had such love for all his children, and I ached that this wonderful man was now broken, confused, and worried for his entire family. Allen's eyes looked tired, there were deep worry lines on his forehead, and he seemed far older than I remembered. Many times I had seen his shoulders shake with sobbing because Zachary was dead or had caught him pensively standing at the window with his hands shoved deeply into his pockets. I saw him struggle with chores that Zachary had helped him with and watched him stand in the doorway of our son's room with a wistful look on his face.

Stepping away from my self-absorbed pain and seeing my husband's sorrow, I couldn't tell if it hurt more to suffer myself or to helplessly watch the heartbreak of someone I dearly loved. I wanted to end his agony but could do nothing to make it stop. I couldn't even make it tolerable, for Zachary's death was unfixable and irreversible.

Later that night the house got quiet and I slipped outside, as I did on many evenings. Flipping on the porch light and leaning against the support column, I stood and deeply inhaled the cool, crisp autumn air with an odd mix of sadness and gratefulness.

It was the first of many birthdays on which we would remember Zachary without his presence. How I missed him that night.

I used to thank him time and time again for mowing the lawn, watching a baby, or stacking wood. How I appreciated him taking a cake out of the oven, lugging in the groceries, or running an errand. I used to genuinely say, "Thanks, sonny! I don't know what I would do without you!"

Now I know.

With great heaviness, I stood on the porch like the brokenhearted father of the prodigal son, looking down the lonely road and straining my eyes against the shadows. Where was my boy? What was he doing? In the vast dark sky, the stars twinkled, and I wondered if Zachary could see them from where he was. Did he ever miss us? Did he ever think of us?

Starting to shiver from the chilly evening air and growing tired of this painful ritual, I wearily turned from the thick blackness. Most moms would flip off the porch light, gratefully relieved because everyone was safely in for the night. They would step into the warm house, close the door behind themselves, and securely lock the door.

Not me.

On these pensive nights, I leave the porch light on as a tribute to my son's life. A simple gesture, perhaps to the world, or maybe just for me, to show that one family member is not safely home where he belongs. As a symbol of our expectancy, the porch light glows in hopeful anticipation, and I in wistful fantasy, that Zachary can see it and know that we lovingly remember him, dearly miss him, and always are mindful of a joyous reunion.

Dear God,

I thank You for the life of this child, for I was blessed with the honor of enjoying him for sixteen years. Please keep the treasured memories of his childhood vibrant as sparkling jewels in my mind to be treasured forever.

2 1

SLEEPLESS

I will lie down and sleep in peace,
for you alone, O Lord,
make me dwell in safety.

Psalm 4:8

The problem with pain's marathon is that there is no finish line in sight. I couldn't be sure if I was at mile twenty-four or mile 240, nor could I tell for certain whether I was closer to the start of the race or nearer to the end. While others were ahead of me and many more behind, in this race set before me, I was the solitary runner, exhausted, out of breath, and oblivious to anything but my burning lungs and weary legs. Having no choice but to continue the repetitive, automated motions of progress and no place to go but onward, I just kept running past the unchanging scenery, fully focused on the hope of seeing the colorful, flapping flags of the finish line around the next bend. I raced, not to win, but to finish, for this marathon would have no winner's circle, no blue ribbon, and no trophy. There won't be cheering crowds, no autographs, and no cameras flashing. Only a finish line. A glorious finish line. And a chance to finally lie down and rest.

In a heartbeat, on any given day, I could get lost in sorrow. Memories of Zachary startled and ambushed me in the most unlikely places—the kitchen, the grocery store, the laundry room, the garage. Like a child with sloppy untied shoelaces, I trip over sorrow when I least expect it and, each time, the stumbling brings me sadness.

Grief is a painful measurement of love and the high price we pay for having valued someone. If I give grief an inch, it will take a mile; for once I start crying, I likely won't be able to stop. On most days, I concentrated on staying busy and focused my full attention on the immediate needs of my family. Storing up the heartache, I tried disregarding grief's leering threats to grow worse by being ignored. I moved sadness to the back burner to simmer and thicken and dealt instead with the soup kettles in front that were bubbling and threatening to overflow and burn. The dying was temporarily set aside for the sake of the living.

As the day wound down, the children were put to bed and the last of the chores were completed. The business of the day and the distractions of my responsibilities ceased, leaving the house quiet and dark. It was then that I punched out on my time card and headed for our bedroom, fully knowing that I could rein back my composure no longer.

Nighttime was no longer my friend. Just as surely as the long shadows know when it is their quiet time to slip in and settle down, death waited for me each evening in every corner of our bedroom. Keeping the promises I made during the day to privately return to my sorrow, I climbed into bed and pulled my favorite quilt high up around my neck. Submissively, I sensed that this nighttime routine was the only way to get through the pain, and I suspected that I needed to use this time wisely. Since I longed for perfectionism in my mourning and wanted to accomplish it correctly, I knew no better way to grieve than to give Zachary my complete and full attention. This grief was the last and final gift I could give him, and I feared that the day would come when the sorrow would end and I would be left with nothing to offer.

As if unlocking a padlocked gate, I swung my mind open on rusty squeaking hinges and received every sad part of my son's death. With tears unrestrained, I dwelt on each precious memory of his life, replayed with great detail the events on the day of his death, and spiraled chaotically through sadness, guilt, and confusion. When I tired of this routine and greatly longed for sleep, I thought of Zachary's face, his mannerisms, and his laugh. I then made a mental list of all the reasons why I loved him and read that list over and over again.

Many times during those dark, torturous nights, I deeply longed for spiritual and physical rest to restore my body and spirit. It was impossible to relax when my pain throbbed like an old knee injury that had been aggravated by the wear of the day. Allen, listening to my deep crying, often had to calm me as one soothingly rocks a restless, colicky baby who cannot be consoled. Perhaps he wondered if I would ever be okay. Maybe he worried that he had lost his wife as well as his son. As he shared in my pain, I was so grateful for his tender comfort during those long tormenting nights.

The darkness had much to teach me, and I tried to be a patient, willing student. As I learned to endure the long nighttime hours, I perhaps even accepted them as some of my best grieving experiences. I spent many stretches of time in prayerful conversations with God, while during many more, I did little other than bask in the comfort of His presence next to me.

Sleep finally came along with the prayerful hope that God could be trusted to provide a fresh portion of mercies for each new morning. And always there was hope that the sun would rise with an easier day.

Dear God,

I hear Your comforting voice the clearest during the night as I lie in the stillness of my room and grieve my son's death. Please salvage my life and renew my heart, for I want to deeply know and be known by You.

2 2

THANKSGIVING

But I trust in your unfailing love;
my heart rejoices in your salvation.
*I will sing to the L*ORD,
for he has been good to me.

Psalm 13:5–6

Thanksgiving was coming, and I dreaded the theme of togetherness. Every nostalgic movie and holiday TV commercial boasted a picturesque extended family pleasantly gathered around a heavily laden banquet. From gray-haired elders to grinning toothless babies in high chairs, relatives of many ages made the dinner table complete. But for our family and others experiencing loss, when we were all together, we most noticed that we weren't.

Thanksgiving Day arrived. The turkey was roasted, the rolls were carefully browned, and the sweet potatoes came out of the oven picture-perfect. As I admired the feast, I missed Zachary. I missed him picking the skin off the turkey and burning his fingers because he was too impatient to wait for it to cool. I missed him slicing the banana bread, swiping his finger in the mashed potatoes, and using far too much whipped cream on his pumpkin pie.

I didn't feel much like giving thanks. I didn't feel much like listening to or creating elaborate prayers of gratefulness. I had prized Zachary and felt rich of great treasure, wealthy in love. Now his death made me feel like a pauper, poor and needy, as if someone had come and stolen something precious to me.

Suddenly I felt guilty for my self-pity and lack of appreciation. Of course I missed my son, and no, I did not deserve to lose him, but neither had I ever done anything to merit having him in the first place. Zachary had been God's good gift to me, and I had enjoyed sixteen years with him. Every day of each of those years had been filled with a rich and beautiful love.

I forced myself to give thanks, for I was still as blessed as I had ever been. There were numerous things to be grateful for, including each of the remaining children who God had given me. These young ones of various ages were now peeling crunchy skin off the turkey, stirring the punch, and requesting extra cookies. Their earnest voices were offering to set the table and presenting beautiful childlike prayers to heaven. It would be a shame if grief blinded me from their presence or if self-pity kept me from appreciating and treasuring these dear, sweet faces glowing in the warmth around the table.

I thought about these children now. Losing one child had shaped me into a more appreciative and devoted parent, and I had become more protective of their emotional well-being. I worried about their hearts.

I considered how it might feel for the children to be different from their peers or to be identified as the sibling of someone who had taken his own life. I wondered if they still felt as if they fit in with their friends who had little if any experience with death and quite possibly none with suicide. I wondered if they were frustrated by their grief, angry that Zachary had abandoned them, or confused about their emotions.

Were the children angry at God because their brother had died or puzzled by those who said this death surely was God's will? Were they sad that they hadn't said good-bye, worried that they may have done something to contribute to his depression, or feeling guilty for wanting to get on with their lives? Were the children jealous of the consuming attention we continued to give Zachary's death or resentful of the fact that at times we appeared to think more about the child we had lost than about the children still living?

I hoped we had not elevated Zachary to a pedestal far higher than he had attained in life or had given him a halo of virtues far beyond his human personality. Zachary deserved no more than his fair share of emotional space in my heart, and I daily put great effort into the process of not letting him sap the emotional energy that rightly deserved to be shared by all the children.

Praying intently for God's wisdom and guidance, I refused to smother the children or put undue pressure on them to appear polished and perfect so that others would be assured of my success as a parent. None of the children would be required to take Zachary's place or magically make up for this sorrow with exalted achievements. I purposed to give each child the freedom to choose his or her own path, realizing that this reflection would be on them and not on my parenting skills.

I earnestly prayed that all of the children had learned the great lesson that nothing would ever be solved by a self-inflicted death and that we would desperately ache for them if they died. As they matured and saw life becoming unmanageable, I prayed they would take responsibility to change the things they did not like in their lives and search for help and options when troubles arose.

These beautiful children, boys and girls of many ages with unique gifts and talents, ultimately belonged to God. They each were on loan to our family from Him, and I would trust the ultimate Father to heal every one differently in His own time. I had already witnessed the children's wounded hearts becoming more sensitive and appreciative toward their family and friends, and I would continue to pray that they would grow into tender adults who would willingly minister with compassion to a hurting world. Courageous and strong, their eager faces beamed brightly with individual passion, simple everyday excitements, and dreams for the future. They were my true heroes. I knew that my own restoration to health was largely, but not solely, based on theirs.

On this Thanksgiving, I slowly looked at the dear faces around my table. We had Jesus, each other, and our freedom. We had a loving community, a warm house, and plenty of provisions. I could pout and mourn over the child I had lost or be thankful for the opportunity of enjoying the many blessings surrounding me today and in the years to come.

My soul was refreshed and as I calmly filled my plate with the steaming, lavish holiday foods, God's goodness continued to satisfy me with gratitude and contentment. Death was teaching me how to live.

Dear God,

Please guard the hearts of my children and help them not to abandon their faith. I continually strive to imitate Your parenting. Please give me insight to teach each child how to live and wisdom to satisfy every emotional need.

23

UNDERSTOOD

*Praise be to the God and Father of our Lord Jesus Christ, the
Father of compassion and the God of all comfort, who comforts
us in all our troubles, so that we can comfort those in any trouble
with the comfort we ourselves have received from God.*

2 Corinthians 1:3–4

My eyes saw things I had never noticed before: handmade crosses on the sides of interstates, obituaries in the local newspapers, well-groomed cemeteries lovingly decorated with artificial flowers, and funeral homes I had vaguely driven past dozens of times. I was learning that grief is a universal part of being human and that people everywhere endure tremendous loss and triumph over staggering pain every day. I wondered if some of these people might even be driving sadly behind me on the highway or in the next aisle of the grocery store absentmindedly pushing their carts while trying to decide what groceries they needed.

My radar screen detected deaths of children in newspapers, magazines, and on TV in a way I never had noticed before. In my

community, someone who had lost a child reached out to me. This
introduction led me to meet others, and I stepped hesitantly into this
new subculture, gaining a circle of new friends as I was welcomed
with intimacy and empathy. I felt safe behind this fence where few
would enter, drawn to this world of suffering as new friendships were
forged in the fires of shared emotion.

All sideswiped by tragedy in different ways, we returned to our
pain and relived it, and in this way, both provided and accepted
healing. By speaking our children's names and admitting they had
died, we were in the same breath acknowledging that they lived and
the telling brought our children back to life for those few moments.
We were in awe of each other's strength, fully respecting the fact that
we had each endured the very worst day of our lives. It was a small
comfort to know that no other day could ever be that bad.

I imagined what it would feel like to lose your child to an accident,
a birth defect, or an illness and found myself envying people who had
lost their children to anything but suicide. I felt horrible for comparing
loss and had no intention of diminishing or devaluing one kind of
death over another, but still, wouldn't it be easier to know that your
child had died against his will and not by his own hand? Wouldn't it be
more peaceful to imagine your child's final moments full of anything
but misery and his plans for a self-imposed death?

Even so, the result was the same for all who had lost a child far
too soon—the daily pain was no less consuming, the dark evening
hours were no less troubling, and the dreams for the future no less
haunting. All of us who had buried a child were living lives that were
considered by most to be a parent's worst nightmare.

Losing a child taught me more about suffering than any book,
professor, or class ever could. Living with sorrow made me treasure

life's joy, and feeling the pain of this world made me appreciate its beauty. I have a deeper appreciation for all my loved ones as well as a greater interdependency on those who are an important part of my life. I have learned firsthand how quickly it can be too late, how very fragile people are, and how nobody is guaranteed an earthly tomorrow.

I view life's problems from a new perspective: long lines at the grocery store, spilled milk, and muddy puddles on the kitchen floor are trivial and irrelevant. I waste none of my precious energy on insignificant difficulties but instead have renewed focus on valuing all that extends into the eternal. I vow to be more transparently dependent on God, for He will never forsake or abandon me in my darkest hour. I had proof of that.

I deeply appreciate the friendship of those who have lost a child, for they have not hidden themselves and their stories away. They eagerly stepped into my world to welcome me into theirs. They willingly shared their journeys of pain and listened intently to mine. I felt ministered to and greatly blessed. This idea of passing along the baton intrigued me and planted seeds in my own mind about how I might do the same.

Could God use me to reach out to others just as He effectively worked through these friends? Could He even use Zachary's story to help those suffering from a suicide loss? I hardly felt effective or prepared and barely appeared strong or influential. Yet throughout the Bible, God had used unlikely and improbable people to boldly perform great tasks for His glory. Although David was an adulterer, Moses was a murderer, and Rahab was a prostitute, these and others were called and equipped by God to courageously lead others and save lives despite their human shortcomings.

Could I do that? Was I willing?

I tucked away my ideas with an eager willingness to see where God might lead me.

Dear God,

Thank You for heroes who have walked this journey ahead of me with strength and courageous living and now nurture those who know loss. They bless me with their outstretched hands and pull me toward healing and wholeness.

2 4

I AM A SURVIVOR

*Consider it pure joy, my brothers, whenever you face trials of
many kinds, because you know that the testing of your faith
develops perseverance. Perseverance must finish its work so that
you may be mature and complete, not lacking anything.*

James 1:2-4

The survivor of a plane crash, shipwreck, earthquake, or any other
monumental life-threatening crisis experiences severe, devastating
physical loss and an ongoing challenge of basic survival. Life jolts to
a screeching halt; nothing but survival matters. By nature, a survivor
must be instinctively smart and courageous in the face of intense pain
and discomfort. The person must improvise and then immediately—
through trial and error—learn coping skills upon which life depends.
Obviously, it makes perfect sense that a loved one left behind by a
suicide is called a suicide survivor.

I deeply longed to meet other suicide survivors, hear their
stories, and glean from their experiences. Time and education
convinced me that others with this painful tragedy must be "out

there somewhere." I resolved to search them out for I was in desperate need of a mentor.

Having little expectation and even less expertise, I plunged in to start a monthly support group for suicide survivors in my community. I simply put an ad in the paper, hung a sign on the front door of my church, and brewed a pot of hot coffee. On that first night, I was humbled and amazed to watch twelve survivors from differing walks of life nervously enter a quiet Sunday school room with downcast eyes and shoulders hunched, as if weary from pushing their wheelbarrows of painful sadness in front of them. Overcoming fear and stigma, we bravely introduced ourselves and then sat around a table and shared our stories.

The group grew as people came out of the woodwork. Whether losing a parent, grandparent, child, spouse, friend, or sibling, we spoke the unspeakable without editing or omission, trying to make sense of each deliberately chosen death. There was no way to grieve these tragedies without simultaneously analyzing and agonizing over the reasons for their dying. We each had an excessive need to tell our story and took turns talking about gruesome things we never should have seen, barely cringing as the stinging words rolled off our tongues.

Suicide survivors are forever tormented about having had guns in their homes, knives in their kitchens, ropes in their garages, and pills in their bathrooms. We gently reminded each other that our loved ones were in a haze of determination and agony, and regardless of what was available, they easily could have misused something else to end their lives.

Standard talk included the compassionate repetition of "You did the best you could," "They made a bad choice," and "It was not your fault." If I could easily acknowledge that my new friends within this support group were innocent of their loved ones' deaths, surely I could acknowledge the same about myself.

Having joined a club none of us wanted to become a member of, we were magnetically drawn to each other in an atmosphere of shared friendship. The isolation had been lifted; I was not alone. Many suicide survivors had walked before me on this dark, unknown journey of pain and confusion. They had blazed a trail ahead of me in the cold, blinding blizzard, and I was following their footsteps, gratefully stepping in the deep tracks of their boots. Seeing other suicide survivors standing alive, breathing, and functioning gave me hope that I, too, would endure.

As I continued to promote and facilitate this monthly support group, the people within it literally helped save my life. I felt intimately known by these new friends who never tried to cheer me up and never rushed me through my grief. They understood the intensity of my confusion, the depth of my hurt, and the complexity of Zachary's death. They carried me tenderly through my tragedy, bore a share of my burden, and even helped me learn to laugh again.

As kindred spirits, we faltered together with no road map, the blind leading the blind, stumbling together down a rocky road that none of us chose to be on. Leaning on each other for support to rebuild our shattered lives, we tripped into holes we didn't see coming, and plodded on ground we no longer trusted to be stable. We were all discovering that, while at times we were consumed by pain, we did not have to be defined by it. Thankful to have obtained this help we so greatly needed, we found our strength coming from a place deep within us and from God who is far beyond us, and only wished our loved ones had somehow done the same.

On my weak days when I couldn't even help myself, I wondered why I was bold enough to suppose that I had any comfort or wisdom to offer others. Still, I did not want Zachary's suicide to be forgotten or my pain hidden away as useless. Although my insight was limited and my knowledge incomplete, I did possess the one true comfort that is found in Jesus Christ and earnestly wanted to pass this powerful message of hope onward to any who would welcome it.

I am not a trained therapist, have no certificates stating a degree, nor framed diplomas with letters behind my name. I never would have chosen to endure a child's suicide death, but I have, and this life experience is like a scout badge. I did not want to earn it or step up to the platform to receive it. Certainly, I did not want to grab a needle and sew this badge onto my shirt for the entire world to see. I have lost and now understand loss; I have suffered and now understand suffering. My badge is proof of this, and it qualifies me to help others in a way few can.

Perhaps we can heal our difficult experiences when we use them to help others in similar situations. The recovering alcoholic inspires a group of men and holds them accountable. The healed drug addict reaches out to boys who are enticed by the promises of inner-city gangs, and the mother who regrets her abortion ministers to the young girl considering one. These who can honestly stand before hurting people and simply say, "I've been there," have more power to enter into restricted places than those wearing the laminated ID tags required to get into the Pentagon.

Bringing these suicide survivors together once a month to gain insight and comfort from each other brought a new purpose to my life. The only way to restoration was through the pain and there was no place to go but forward. Healing finally seemed attainable on this long and weary journey back to me.

Dear God,

Please equip me to serve and minister to those who are in pain and lead them to healing, pointing them to the hope that is only available through You. Please redeem this tragedy and change lives with this story so that my suffering will not be in vain.

2 5

TEACHING OTHERS

I will boast all the more gladly about my weaknesses, so that Christ's
power may rest on me. For when I am weak, then I am strong.

2 Corinthians 12:9–10

As parents, we attempt to educate our children about life, but
sometimes it is our own children who do the most teaching. In my
case, Zachary provided me with a crash course in suicide and, in
doing so, taught me that nothing is ever so impossible, so despairing,
or so hopeless that a self-inflicted death could be the answer. I am
a different person because of this education—so much less stagnant
and fuller of knowledge—because suicide never barges into lives
without changing the ones affected by it.

As a young mother, I had sought out Christian resources and
educated myself on raising children. Attentively, I had listened to
radio broadcasts, heeded our pastor's teachings, and gleaned wisdom
from experienced moms. I had watched TV shows, read magazines,
and studied parenting books. Together, Allen and I had actively
warned our children about talking to strangers, taught them how to

choose appropriate friends, and discussed the dangers of drugs and alcohol. With our older children, we had even addressed difficult issues like pornography, sex, and divorce. We felt we had done our best to educate and prepare our children for the luring temptations in the world today.

The bizarre thing is, although I felt forewarned and considered myself to be an educated, vigilant parent, I don't remember any of those respectable Christian teachers or resources ever teaching me, imploring me, or begging me to discuss suicide with my children. Because of this, I had simply never considered it to be a risk that might jeopardize my family. I had no reason to deem it a threat.

Why is that? Do parenting experts believe that if you are following their teaching and doing all the "right things" to raise your child, then suicide would never occur and hence you don't need to even worry about it or mention it to your child? Does the myth exist that talking about suicide might put the idea into naïve minds? Or does our society have such a fearful stigma surrounding suicide that it is a taboo subject better left unspoken?

Regardless, many parents similar to myself have either never been taught to discuss suicide or are far too fearful to say the *S* word to their children.

I was on a mission to change that.

Within our local rural community where it is easy to know and be known by others, my son's death sometimes came up in casual conversation at the ballpark, in the store, and after the morning worship service. Whenever I felt comfortable, I shared facts concerning his death. This was far easier to do than it had been in earlier days, because now I was outfitted with a motive. Every time parents of preteens or teenagers heard Zachary's story, I was passionate about adding a piece of education to the conversation that might encourage parents to be bold enough to talk with their children about suicide.

Who doesn't remember being a teenager? There are cheerleading squads to try out for, proms to worry about, and final exams to pass. There are rules and deadlines, best friends and bullies, stressful decisions about the future, and members of the opposite sex. Life can be chaotic, confusing, and sometimes altogether bewildering.

In the turbulent brains of impulsive and spontaneous teenagers, the fleeting thought of suicide may already be there. After all, in today's world of instant media, teenagers are not immune to this topic and hear it mentioned frankly in movies or in the news. Teens are easily influenced and peer oriented. If one teenager hears that another person, especially their age, chose suicide when life's demands became crushing, it would make sense that an impressionable teenager could easily weigh the value of following that example when his or her own life becomes overwhelming.

Suicide is no doubt a tough subject—and not much fun to talk about, but bringing up this tough subject on the edge of a teenager's bed in the evening or asking a few honest questions while driving in the car can open the door to a frank discussion. Regardless of whether or not the child appears to be in any emotional trouble, it is not the talk that is the enemy; it is the secrecy that must be feared. An offer of help can be a life preserver to a teen who thinks no one understands his or her despair. One conversation can save a life: "You seem depressed; is anything bothering you?" or "Have you ever felt like hurting yourself?" There is opportunity for education and concern as a parent shares, "Life is hard for me sometimes too," or "Is there anything I can help you with, because I love and care about you?"

Another valuable idea is to take a story from the news about a current suicide and use it as a springboard for diving into a safe discussion. "Why do you think that happened?" or "How do you think the ones left behind felt?" Guiding children to learn, reflect, and exercise wisdom is the key to promoting suicide awareness and prevention.

While they may not always appear to enjoy it, most teenagers truly value significant conversations with adults. When suicide is discussed, a taboo is lifted and the powerful chains of silence and isolation are broken. I grieved many times to imagine all of the conversations that I would have liked to have had with Zachary and often wondered if any of them might have saved his life. The power of one good conversation can never be underestimated.

Perhaps we, as a Christian life-saving community, can also educate our preteens and teenagers to be on the lookout for bullying and depression among their friends. We can warn our children to be observant and nurturing, while teaching them to never turn a deaf ear to any casual joking or serious threat from a friend or acquaintance who might be suicidal.

My world was expanding, and I was learning how prevalent suicide was everywhere, even among Christian families. I had learned things about the mind and the human spirit that I never knew existed, and feeling the weight of this knowledge, I had a responsibility to warn others with this information. Zachary's story needed to be shared, regardless of how difficult it was to advise people on child raising. Maybe warning signs in other families could be identified and safety measures or counseling could be put into practice. Maybe just one teenager would rethink his desperate intention and a life would be saved. My son had given no audible cries for help, but maybe I could now draw attention to his silent requests.

Dear God,

I am fighting the good fight; I will finish this race. I am far stronger than I ever thought I was and able to endure much more than I ever knew. You, my rock and fortress, alone deserve the glory and praise for my survival.

2 6

CHRISTMAS

*Praise be to the L*ORD*,*
for he has heard my cry for mercy.
*The L*ORD *is my strength and my shield;*
my heart trusts in him, and I am helped.

Psalm 28:6

Outside our snug farmhouse, the whipping winter winds were icy and frigid and when I took a breath, the frosty air sent a chilling sharpness into my lungs. Inside, I was cold all the time and wore many layers to alleviate my constant shivering. I could find no warmth for either body or spirit.

Christmas was coming and my lack of enthusiasm was apparent. Braced for the heavy sadness of missing a child who loved the anticipation of this magical season, the world's jolly merriment was a mockery. During the holidays, Zachary had bounced off the walls with suspense and joy. He not only created lists of what he wished for but also made lists of what he planned to purchase for others. Skilled at being in tune with people's interests, he had an amazing ability to watch, listen, and then surprise each person with the exact movie, book, or music CD that he or she had been wanting.

When we ventured to prepare for Christmas and opened the dusty storage boxes of decorations, there was a little bit of Zachary in every one. Slowly and reverently, I pulled out ornaments with lopsided lettering he had crafted in Sunday school, figurines he had thoughtfully purchased for me, and the twinkling lights he had taken off the tree and neatly wrapped up just last year. I lifted the wreath he had hung in glad welcome on our front door, Nativity figures he had carefully arranged in the little wooden stable, and his stocking that I had sewn from snowmen fabric he had chosen.

He should be here, I mourned bitterly. He should be here setting up the Christmas tree with his artistic eye, hanging and rearranging ornaments, lights, and strings of wooden cranberries until everything was just right. He should be sneaking around under the tree shaking the gifts bearing his name, helping me buy the holiday ham, and reminding me to make sugar cookies.

But he wasn't.

Christmas Day arrived with great heaviness, yet we were courageous and brave for the children. Sitting on the braided rug in the family room in front of the tree together, Allen and I put batteries into new toys, helped tear sticky plastic off candy canes, and happily echoed joy at every present that was eagerly opened and enjoyed. As the radio played Christmas carols in the background and our wood stove radiated warmth and comfort, we kept the day positive and happy, not wanting to linger on how sad it was without Zachary—but everybody sensed it.

Evening finally came and the younger children, blissfully content, soon fell asleep in their beds clutching their new stuffed animals and prized toys. I pushed aside the stray scraps of torn wrapping paper, the boxes from new cameras and electronic gadgets, and the many tags happily cut off the older children's new clothing. Sitting in the dark watching the little lights twinkle on our Christmas tree, I listened to the radio for company, held Zachary's limp stocking in my lap, and let the tears come as I thought about how much I missed him.

The beautiful story of Luke 2 that we think about so much during this time of year entered my mind, and I opened my Bible to reread it. Mary, the chosen mother of Jesus, had delivered, loved, and nurtured a little boy. She had stitched his clothes, prepared his dinner, and swept away the dirt tracked in from his muddy sandals. She had cringed when he skinned his knee, worried when he was out late at night, and proudly watched him grow into a tender, sensitive young man. Mary knew what it was like to lovingly invest her heart and life into a child. I felt a kinship to her now, for she also knew what it was like to watch her child suffer a violent death and then disappear from her daily life.

The Bible says that Mary, like sentimental mothers throughout time, stored these precious treasures from her child's life deeply in her heart and pondered them. After Jesus died and went away, it was these memories that soothed her heartbreaking sorrow. As she went about her daily tasks, kneading her bread or tending to her vegetables, she pondered. When she strode back and forth to the well to fetch water on the dusty roads or tossed restlessly during the many lonely, sleepless nights, she pondered.

Mary loved and lost. She yearned to look deeply into her son's eyes, ached to touch Him again, and longed for just one more lively conversation. I was comforted by the thought that Mary walked before me and greatly knew the pain of losing a son. She lived with the promise of seeing Jesus again and always, until her own life dwindled and her days on earth diminished, she pondered. Mary, the truest of all mothers, has already been reunited with her son. I am holding out for that same glad day.

For no particular reason, this Christmas while in the grocery store, I purchased a box of clementine oranges, and although I wasn't familiar with these little gems, I thought the children might enjoy trying them during the holidays. I decided to take a hint from the pioneers of long ago and placed one small orange in each of the children's stockings along with their other goodies. The result on Christmas morning was delightful. Each child was surprised both with this sweet treat as well as humored with the knowledge that long ago, this may have been one of only a few extravagances to be received on Christmas morning. Several happy voices cried, "Can we do this again next year?" and it warmed my heart to realize that this new tradition, which Zachary would never know or be a part of, could bring happiness to our family in future years.

Christmas was soon over and the boxes of ornaments and decorations were once again carefully packed and put into storage. As the local stores put their seasonal merchandise on clearance and the radio resumed playing its regular music, I felt a measure of both peace and relief that we had made it through this difficult season. In the past we had enjoyed many wonderful Christmases with Zachary, and somehow—I suppose mostly through trial and error—we would learn to endure many more without him. By keeping numerous treasured, timeworn traditions and by being open-minded enough to create new ones, we would welcome the holidays. And always, we would remember Zachary.

Dear God,

You, the humble Christ child, grew up and lived with suffering, yet pleased the Father with Your life. May Your face shine upon me and find pleasure in the ways of my heart as I seek to accomplish the plan set before me.

2 7

HOPEFUL OF HEAVEN

I love you, O LORD, my strength.

Psalm 18:1

I always assumed that I would die when I was old and gray, leaving my children and grandchildren behind to continue the family legacy and then pass it on to their loved ones. I would step into heaven first and my loved ones would remain behind to add many more branches to the family tree. The scheme of things as I understood it was: grandparents die, parents die, and then children die.

But things had not worked out as I anticipated.

For many months I mourned that my son's life had ended without his carrying out the plans that God had intended for his existence. I mourned that Zachary had chosen to leave before his time was up and now neither he, nor I, nor any of his friends or family members would get to see what might have happened in the months and years to come.

I thought a lot about Zachary dwelling in heaven—that mysterious and wonderful place I've not yet seen—and I wondered if he missed us or if his strange new world ever appeared as foreign to him as my new world seemed to me. Perhaps during Zachary's quiet times in heaven, he paused to remember his former life and was as comforted by his memories of us as we were soothed by our memories of him.

Upon Zachary's entrance into heaven, I believe God gave him a new role specifically designed for his person, a tailor-made function created exclusively for him that far outweighed whatever he had been meant to accomplish here on earth. I could easily imagine my son attentively taking direct orders from God Himself and then walking the streets of gold as he cheerfully accomplished whatever tasks he was asked to do. If heaven is a diversified community with each member participating according to his or her specific talents, then my extraordinary son is contributing by using his own gifts in a brand-new way. Zachary LaBonte is not dead; he is alive in heaven—more beautifully alive than he ever was here on this earth! And I am fully confident that if he were offered the opportunity to return to the meager life he knew here in this sinful, difficult world, he would quickly smile and reply with a confident, "No thanks!"

I loved imagining Zachary bowing down in worship before God the Father. My own son had gotten a head start on adoring and praising his Creator! My child had achieved something I was still dreaming of. What a thought!

As my children grew, there was great competition in one child succeeding before the others. Whether it was riding a two-wheeler or elbowing to grab the last cookie, cooperation dissolved as antagonistic sparks flew. Whether it was snatching the window seat in the van or being the first to mow the lawn or own a vehicle, sibling rivalry sometimes trumped friendship.

I smiled to think of Zachary reaching heaven before his family, laughing like he did when he was the first to reach a scenic peak during a hike, the first to splash into the swimming pool, or the first to discover an especially bountiful cluster of ripe strawberries. I could imagine him motioning wildly with his arms and eagerly urging us along. I could envision him insisting that we quickly join him with the glad call, "Come! Hurry! You've got to see this!"

When Zachary was a little boy, I often read Bible storybooks to him that contained glorious pictures of heaven—golden mansions, pearly gates, and celestial angels, but these portrayals were entirely inadequate. My artistic son is now admiring the beauty and complexity of heaven and perhaps even shaking his head and laughing because we greatly underestimated the beauty and perfection there. Happy and purposeful, the beautiful surroundings are so much more wonderful than he ever imagined. The glory of heaven takes his breath away every day.

Although I am longing to see my heavenly Father when this physical life is over, I also exist as a human mother and comfort myself with daydreams of what it will be like to set eyes on my son again. When I wake up in glory and see Zachary, will we run into each other's arms and embrace with laughter and weeping, needing no words to restore our relationship? Will the bond of our love trump the measure of time? I am counting the days until I can look deeply into his eyes and see for myself that everything is truly all right.

I can't wait to stand beside Zachary as we join heaven's vast crowds in glad worship of our Creator. I can't wait to share a hymnbook, to sense him tall and proud beside me, and to feel his warm breath in song as I join my voice with his in glad praise to our Father.

Zachary is in good hands now, far better hands than he ever had been in on earth. He is home now—where we all ultimately belong at the end of this journey—and enthusiastically waiting for us, eager to give a tour and excited to show off the splendor he has experienced.

Perhaps Zachary is saving seats for us, reserving room, roping off a tiny section of glory's pews with a brilliant red cord and a kind, apologetic whisper to those who were preparing to sit. I can hear him saying, "Sorry. I am saving these seats for my family."

Perhaps he is eagerly helping God prepare a home for us, earnestly sweeping off the front porch, and maybe even planting a few bright pink geraniums in front of my mansion in glad welcome. I can envision him laying the shovel aside, brushing the earthy soil off his fingers, and then leaning there against the porch railing with his hands shoved deeply into his jean pockets. He has a glorious smile on his contented face and looks down the road, waiting with joyful anticipation for his family members to arrive. And as surely as my son is expecting me, I am waiting for my Zachary.

Dear God,

Please help me live with eternity in view, for my life is but a vapor. Fill me with contentment while I long for that moment when I will see my son again. It is a comfort to know he is no longer in pain, but gloriously satisfied with You.

2 8

I AM HEALING

*But those who hope in the L*ORD *will renew their strength,*
they will soar on wings like eagles; they will run and
not grow weary, they will walk and not be faint.

Isaiah 40:31–32

More often than not, the days were turning mild. The icy snow was melting and running like little rivers into the ground, taking with them the last of winter's chill. Expectant robins chirped happily and little, green spears of daffodils poked hesitantly from the warming soil. Spring was bringing hope as I, too, waited for renewal and growth.

In this world where we compare medicine labels to make sure our cold symptoms, headaches, and heartburn will disappear quicker than they could with another product on the shelf, it goes against our human nature to wait. As busy people, we want to erase discomfort with a tiny pill, a doctor's consultation, a quick fix, or an emergency prayer rushed to heaven's gates.

The Bible challenges us to wait upon the Lord to find new strength. Could it really be that strength arrives when we do nothing other than wait? Just wait? How bizarre that I could do little to ease my suffering except cling to the promise that help would arrive in its own due time. Nothing in nature or in grieving can be rushed. Just as a tender rosebud is destroyed when forced open, I would have to wait calmly and let time, nature, and God do their curative work.

I was the only one who could choose what my reaction to my son's death would be, and I was determined to do more than simply survive. I was not about to let "grieving, sad mother" be my permanent role, for somewhere in the last few months, my survival instincts had kicked in and I wanted to productively thrive. Zachary had made his decision to die; I made mine to live.

Some of the darkness was lifting, the heaviness rising, and my white-knuckled, almost choking grip on my children's safety was slowly relaxing. Parenting solely out of fear was exhausting and constrictive. Their lives were not solely for my pleasure and comfort, and like blinking, yellow fireflies in a thick mason jar, my children had been safe but perhaps not free. Unscrewing the cap poked jaggedly with air holes, I felt myself relaxing and giving their little wings the freedom to be themselves with my true, generous blessing instead of with reluctant, cautious permission.

I had been a stranger in a foreign land long enough and was tired of misunderstanding the language and struggling with the street signs. I wanted to return to my hometown and resume those things about my life that had brought me pleasure and joy—specifically, the role of foster parenting our state's abused and neglected children, a ministry I thoroughly enjoyed.

In the six years prior to Zachary's death, Allen and I had fostered more than twenty children. Zachary had great and tender compassion for these needy little ones who came through our home for various periods of time. He carried the babies, wiped their noses, and played with them on the floor. He winked at the preschoolers and coaxed smiles from the most fearful of faces, often pouring their juice, or taking them outside to be pushed on the swings. Zachary understood that our home was a refuge for these children, and I believe that hearing their sad stories made him understand how blessed he really was.

Allen and I believed that caring for these abused and neglected foster children was a true part of our Christianity, and I loved the challenge and joy of bringing love and healing into their broken and chaotic lives. I made a phone call to the local agency to resume fostering and eagerly waited for my phone to ring.

Soon I was again welcoming the little ones into my home. They arrived dirty and ill clothed, blinking like little owls in the middle of the night with doubtful eyes and suspicious hearts. The world had hurt them, and they had been abandoned by the ones whom they should have been able to trust. These little children would always be affected by the choices of their caregivers and would forever be linked to a sad family legacy. I felt a kinship with them, for they, too, were disappointed, confused, and unsure of their future. Welcoming little hearts as wounded as mine, I gathered them eagerly into my arms, for surely we had more in common than anyone recognized.

Although most of the children seemed cautiously optimistic, they were willing to give life another try. Love, good food, and stability taught them how to trust and fanned the dim embers in their eyes into twinkling sparks of playful laughter. Thriving on seemingly little, they were content having their simplest needs met.

Sometimes foster children woke up crying during the night. I would rush to pick them up and offer comfort by rubbing their little backs and stroking their soft heads. As I rhythmically tried to rock away sorrow and heartache, I listened to these little ones trying to catch their breath through their pitiful choking sobs, and thinking of Zachary, wept along in agreement over the sad injustices of the world.

On those pensive nights while the stars twinkled peacefully out in the black sky, I looked out into infinity, watched the trees sway in the nighttime breeze, and felt inside myself a wellspring of hope and healing. Feeling Zachary's blessing, I sat in the same chair where I had rocked him and sang the same lullabies of comfort that he had listened to and loved. These hurting children who were not my own wrapped their little, warm arms tightly around my neck and were comforted by my kindness, just as God's companionship gently soothes and quiets me. As surely as I deeply loved and was drawn to these who were crushed and brokenhearted, so the Father has great compassion on me.

As joy slowly returned to my life, seeping back into the empty spaces of my heart, I was greatly relieved to experience this familiar emotion again. Having feared that I was doomed to sadness, I was pleased to find that joy could dwell in my heart side by side with sorrow. None of my happiness would ever diminish my loss or be a betrayal of my love for Zachary, but rather, finding joy in ministry was evidence that I was totally capable of allowing my life—however raggedy and frayed—to serve others and be a testimony of God's healing power.

Although I wished to magically fix the pain of each foster child's past and transform their current situations, I was a limited individual and could only do what was humanly possible to ease their hurts and show them Christ's love for the space of time they were in our home. As much as I wanted to make an impact in every child's life I encountered, birth or foster, I was humbled to realize that I could neither control any child's future nor expect that my limited amount of influence would affect the choices of their lives.

No, I hadn't been able to keep my own little boy alive and now fully understood that I never possessed the power to succeed at that undertaking. I had only been capable of giving a child the best of myself and would do that now for these foster children by infusing them with as much strength and resilience as I could impart. Bathing them with God's love, I can offer security and protection without reservation or regret, fully knowing that my own life will be transformed by giving as much as theirs may be shaped by receiving.

Dear God,

Open my eyes as You refine me in this fire, for I want to gain wisdom from all the lessons You have for me. Spare me no teaching so that I may fully learn from my life experiences. Fuel my passions to love and care for the least of these.

29

GONE ONE YEAR

Now to him who is able to do immeasurably more than all
we ask or imagine, according to his power that is at work
within us, to him be glory in the church and in Christ Jesus
throughout all generations, for ever and ever! Amen.

Ephesians 3:20–21

Zachary had been gone for almost one year, for March 6 was quickly approaching. We were counting the days with considerable fear and dread. It would be a day of deep sorrow for every member of our family as we regrettably recalled Zachary's darkest hour as well as every moment of our blackest day.

The days leading up to the anniversary of Zachary's death were full of torrential rains, as if the heavens themselves were weeping to remember this date and pitying that we would have to relive its horror. The heavy rains left thick mud everywhere and symbolized my life, for on most days, I felt unable to get any traction. I was mired in the agony of Zachary's death while at the same time endeavoring to move forward with joy; neither forward nor reverse brought grip or successful movement. With my wheels spinning in the ruts, I often felt powerless and strangely paused in time, suspended somewhere between the past and my future.

March 6 arrived and our loved ones remembered. They again descended on us as a band of wingless angels with concern, bringing flowers and food along with many sympathetic hugs, cards, and phone calls. Although I drew strength from their love and sincerely appreciated every act of kindness, there was no way to accept the healing without it accentuating the pain. Like rubbing ointment into a wound and feeling the very sting that will eventually cure, the extra doses of kindness ironically reminded us that we had terrible pain that still needed comforting.

On this anniversary of Zachary's first year in heaven, Allen and I visited the cemetery. It was almost spring—the same kind of warm and lovely day our son had died on. We said little as we walked to Zachary's headstone and then stood there near the beautiful black rock we had painfully chosen. I was delighted and comforted to see that the daffodils we had carefully removed from our yard and tenderly transplanted around his headstone were faithfully preparing to bloom, despite their strange, new location.

My son's beautiful name was now on a headstone. While I was pregnant, Allen and I had expectantly pored over baby books, studied meanings, and played with different first-, middle-, and last-name combinations—all the while trying to choose the perfect name for our second son. We confidently decided on Zachary, which means "remembered by God." Excitedly I imagined Zachary Lee LaBonte on his birth certificate and childhood immunization records. How striking that handsome name would appear in calligraphy on a high school diploma or in fine script on a marriage license. How attractive it would look in a classic font on a résumé, a car title, or a mortgage document. Never had I pondered what that beautiful name would look like coldly typed on a police report, an autopsy statement, or a death certificate. Never had I thought to envision how it would look etched deeply into a black headstone that now stands quietly in a rural church cemetery.

I looked at Zachary's birth and death dates now and noticed the hyphen that signified all of the living that occurred between those two moments in time. What was the measure of a man? What factors determined whether someone had lived successfully or not? Many people live a long physical life but barely encourage or influence others because their negativity, selfishness, or lack of concern causes them to walk parallel to those nearby. Others live only a short while on this earth but are remembered forever because they intertwined themselves with family and neighbors, radiated God's personality, and touched lives with their extraordinary gifts of kindness and humility.

Zachary was a tender soul. He was an incredible son, a fantastic brother, and above all else, a beloved child of God who will be remembered for his warm gentleness, silly humor, and generous love. His dramatic and somewhat sensational death was not his whole life, nor was it in character with his personality. One act of desperation to save himself from further pain could never cancel out the wise and godly choices he made throughout his life. Although there was something vitally important about my son at the end of his life that I might never know, I would focus instead on everything about his heart that I was certain of. I would not, nor would I let anyone else, invalidate Zachary's character or define him by one poor choice.

The cemetery was peaceful, reverent of our thoughts. I looked past my son's headstone with a curious interest as if just noticing the intense green of the freshly cut cemetery grass, the music of the songbirds, and the hopeful budding trees near Zachary's grave. In the distance, I heard the clamor of migrating geese that had bravely left their warm southern havens in eager flight to return home. The breeze smelled promising with an earthy dampness of life and renewal.

"He's over his suicide, you know," Allen said, standing quietly within touch. "The despair and confusion; he's way past that. He's nothing but completely satisfied with God."

I pondered this new thought. Just as winter had ceased and the earth with all its creatures were over the past season of barren coldness, Zachary, too, had moved on with a new purpose. He was now concerned with bigger and better pursuits.

For a year, I had envisioned my child mired in emotional pain, and it had been torture to me as his mother. What a thought that the last troubled hours and the last desperate minutes of Zachary's life were long gone. He had been raised to heaven, straight into the arms of Jesus. There, in a quiet place, perhaps on a quiet bench, God had lovingly put His arm around my son's weary shoulders and explained each confusing notion away.

Safe with Jesus, my child was no longer hurting, and no longer agonizing over a frail part of his humanness. How wonderful it must feel to have the weight of this world off his shoulders, to be free from the pain and struggles of this life. For whatever it was that the world couldn't offer, my son was no longer in need and I rejoiced that nothing could hurt him again.

I stood in my husband's tender embrace, feeling deeply understood by this dear man who loved Zachary as much as I did and who held my life together as surely as he held me now. Many years ago, Allen had sat beside me on that blessed afternoon when Zachary was born and had continued to sit beside me for each piano recital and Christmas program. He was the one who stood beside me when our son's body was being lowered into a bleak, dark hole and who stood beside me now in front of our son's headstone. He walked beside me faithfully, always, and I knew he would continue to do so for every step of this journey.

We had grieved Zachary's death very differently in the past year, but the promise to do it together without criticism or accusation had never been broken. Our bond was stronger now than ever, and the petty things that might have annoyed us about each other in the past had faded in light of focusing on survival and keeping our family together. Sharing deeply in pain had produced intimacy, and like two victims surviving a shipwreck, we were bound together with a deep camaraderie.

We had endured one year without Zachary. We had watched the calendar pages turn and the seasons change, and with each had said good-bye to our son a little bit more, letting his death sink into our hearts a little bit deeper. It had taken sixteen years to get to know Zachary, would it now take fifteen more years to get completely used to his being gone? In some kind of a mathematical equation where one number cancels out the other, would the idea of his being dead for the same amount of time he had lived bring us full circle back to a life without Zachary?

Like weary, satisfied hikers victoriously reaching a mountaintop vista, we were using this day to turn around and observe our journey of the past arduous year. As if we stood at a sign marked "scenic overlook," there was a respectful and invigorating quality to our view down the mountain, for although we were blistered and exhausted, we could visualize how far we had come. As children of a faithful God, we had never walked alone. When we had tripped and fallen, our loyal Father had always been there to pick us back up. As the altitude changed and the terrain challenged us, with each step we had breathed in God's grace and exhaled prayers of thanksgiving for His daily strength and provisions. This we would surely continue to do, for it really was the only way we knew to live.

I looked at Zachary's headstone gleaming in the sunshine and let my eyes rest on the ceramic oval photo of his face. Looking deeply into those beautiful green eyes, I was saddened to think that I would never again see his dear facial expressions nor again be warmed by that friendly signature single nod of his head. Every face within our family would continue to grow older while Zachary's would forever remain sixteen.

I pulled out the wet paper towel I had brought with me and wiped off the dust that had settled there on his beloved face, just as surely as I used to gently wipe the peanut butter off his little cheeks. This was now the only physical task I could do for Zachary, and it caused me sadness to perform even this simplest of honors.

Cleaning away the grass clippings and dirt, I felt the headstone's smooth coolness under my fingertips and thought of the precious body lying there in the ground under my feet. I noticed that the patch of grass hiding the casket's scar in the ground did not match the color of the native grasses nearby. It seemed the earth had rejected this trauma as much as I. Lingering there at his headstone, I was finally overcome with sadness. I walked away with Allen, taking only my memories and the dirty paper towel with me.

For many months I believed that this cemetery not only held what I desperately needed but also possessed that which was required for my very existence. But now I knew. All that I truly needed was beyond the physical and emotional boundaries of this place. Many times since Zachary's death I had thought my life was over. I had believed I could not continue on. But like a vintage pickup truck that sputters and stammers, life was beginning again.

Finally it was time for Allen and me to leave the cemetery, for we had spent enough time in this place. Ready to return to our family and home, I walked to the parked car with confidence and peace, feeling the spring sun shine warmly on my face.

Climbing inside, I adjusted the passenger mirror and glanced into it to take one more look at the cemetery's reflection behind me. I wanted to be more interested in the future than I was in the past. Turning my eyes to look out the front windshield, I knew I wanted to operate my life by focusing on what was ahead of me, instead of on what was behind.

The tires crunched in the gravel as we drove down the long cemetery driveway. With my focus on the road before me, I left the past where it rightfully belonged and headed forward to the life I chose, the life I knew, the life I loved.

For it was a beautiful day to be alive.

Dear God,

This milestone day is proof that survival is possible. I love You, for You have sustained my life. You have kept Your promises to walk with me through sorrow and for that, I praise Your wonderful works. I remain devoted to You.

DEAR ZACHARY

The memory of the righteous will be a blessing.

Proverbs 10:7

Dear Zachary,

The chaotic heartache over your death did in no way cease at the one-year mark when we drove out of that cemetery. I did not neatly sweep up the turmoil, hang up the dustpan, and continue peacefully with my life. The shock of your suicide was a terrible jolt, and you stayed on my mind every day of the next year. Years three and four found me struggling daily with the grief of your absence as I continued to navigate my new life with deep sighs of regret and sadness.

Now it has been five years, and people ask me, "Does it get easier?" I will admit that five years feels better than three weeks or two months or one year. Perhaps with time—although death remains devastating—it becomes solely yours, somewhat familiar, and even strangely comfortable, like an old, faded, worn coat that fits around your shoulders perfectly, even though you have tired of the style and color and would much prefer to replace it with a more attractive garment.

As surely as you carved your initials on the wooden picnic table in the backyard and on that tree in the woods that was "yours," you left your mark permanently engraved on all who knew you, for always; Z.L.L. will be deeply etched upon my heart.

I am like the schoolteacher who confirms the morning class roster, for regularly I perform a mental roll call of all my children and your name is permanently on that list. For as long as I have life, each of you, near or far, is deeply loved and mindfully pondered each day.

Your brothers have turned into excellent men, your sisters into beautiful young ladies. The children we adopted fill our home with much delight. In five years you have missed so much in your siblings' lives—new cars and motorcycles, military enlistments and career changes, graduations and birthdays. In the years to come, when we rejoice over weddings, cheer for new home purchases, and delight in the arrival of grandbabies, you will be missing even more.

My life is incredibly productive and joyful, yet if I look for it, there is always a dull ache in the bottom of my heart. It hurts during gorgeous winter snowfalls and through deafening summer thunderstorms. It hurts during crisp autumn days and always on those glorious spring mornings.

I had no idea of your pain just as surely as you never could have predicted mine. I will always be sorry for your silent agony, sorry for the times I failed you, and sorry that I was unable to make it all right. Jesus has done that for you now, and I can't wait to see all that you have become in heaven's glory.

Please forgive me, seventy times seven and for as long as it takes, understanding that my human failures and personal shortcomings never meant you pain or harm. I remain in great need of your genuine forgiveness and will be much satisfied on that day when I receive a personal confirmation directly from your lips.

Promise me, please, that you will never forget who we were or what we meant to you. Promise me that even in your glorified heavenliness, you will always remember your loyal human family who eagerly waits and longingly hopes in the promise of seeing you again. Your forever has begun; I am still waiting for mine.

You never set out to teach me about hope, but you did, and I have learned far more than I ever thought I needed to discover. Foremost, I have learned what can happen to a life that has even the smallest measure of hope, and I have learned what can happen to a life that doesn't.

Hope rarely shouts and often whispers. It seldom barges in and frequently knocks softly. Like embers left untended, hope lies quietly, ready to be fanned into sparks that will ignite a roaring fire. Like a dim flashlight that keeps you moving forward as you stumble in the dark, hope can provide just enough light to show you where to place your next foot even when the future looks shadowy and unclear. Hope fervently promises that things will get better, that the journey will get easier, and that one day the pain will soften.

The love and companionship of our Father in heaven who faithfully keeps His promise to always be with us is our constant hope, our loyal hope, and our eternal hope. During the brightest sunny days and on every lonely night, He alone can provide for our every need and satisfy our every longing. You know that now better than I do.

For sixteen years, three months, and twenty-seven days, I did my best to care for you. I was an imperfect mother, yet I adored you, valued you, and watched in awe at the talents you displayed. I loved you just the way you were and watched in pleasure at all you were becoming. I was exceedingly proud of the way you lived.

I thank God for you, my beautiful boy who was quickly becoming a man, a boy who had so many wonderful qualities to offer the world, a boy so normal and yet so altogether extraordinary. I will forever be charmed by your beautiful smile and glorious cheerfulness, be warmed by the endless memories of your wonderful childhood, and be blessed by your kind thoughtfulness. I will always treasure the times you made me laugh, the gifts you chose for me on special occasions, and every drawing you so thoughtfully sketched. It's true; you never know what you've got until it's gone.

At your birth I made a promise that you could never do anything to make me stop loving you. I am keeping that promise, holding to my end of the bargain, even after this one thing that has caused me such suffering. I still and always will love you. I cannot stop.

For many years I believed the worst thing in my life was losing you. Now I know that the worst thing would be to have never known you. I thank God for choosing me to be your mother, for your life brought me much joy and delight. Forever you remain God's good gift to our family.

Always loving you,
Mommy

SURVIVAL GUIDE

Every forty seconds someone in the world dies by suicide. Every forty-one seconds someone is left to make sense of it.

- You are NOT alone. You do not have to suffer by yourself.
- This death is not your fault. While you were influential in your loved one's existence, you are not responsible for a poor choice made to end his or her life. Work to forgive yourself and your loved one for any and all shortcomings.
- Make a list entitled Things I Did Right. Review it often. Focus on the things you did to enrich and bring joy into your loved one's life. It can be very healing.
- Even though you'll never like it, accept that a suicide death leaves you to live with unanswered questions. The why may never completely disappear.

- Permit all overwhelming feelings of anger, guilt, regret, fear, and pain. Do not underestimate or be afraid of their intensity. Strong emotions are a normal and necessary part of the healing process. Confide in a trusted friend. Talk. Talk. Talk. Repeat yourself and your story as often as you need to.
- Guard your marriage and close relationships. Do not play the blame game or push away the ones you most need in your life. Commit to work together toward healing, understanding that everyone's style of grieving will be different.
- God has promised never to forsake you, to walk with you through this storm, and to always keep your head above the raging waters. The suicide death may challenge beliefs you once held or cause you to reexamine your faith. Don't turn your back on God. He is big enough to accept all of your confusion, doubt, and questioning. Talk to Him.
- Spend time in God's Word. Aim to truly understand who God is rather than trying to determine what His role in the death was.
- Be gentle with yourself as you wait for healing on your own personal timetable. Rest, eat well, exercise. Place protective perimeters around your home and your schedule. Simplify your life.
- There is no right or wrong way to grieve—only *your* way. Trust your instincts, for you alone know what you most need.

- Give yourself full permission to focus solely on your loss whenever you need to. Choose a safe spot for personal reflection. Schedule your grief. The routine of a couch, a favorite quilt, and a good cry can be repetitively soothing.
- Your personal relationships may change. Only surround yourself with those who will be unafraid of your grieving and truly supportive in your healing. Accept help when it is offered. Allow yourself to be nurtured.
- Count on there being people who won't know how to deal appropriately with any aspect of suicide. On the other hand, accept any genuine, kind condolences in whatever awkward form they might be offered. Speak the word *suicide* and educate people on how to treat you.
- Seek out other suicide survivors and glean from their stories. Trust that survival is possible. Try a support group. This may be the best strategy for survival.
- Elect to focus on what you can control. Your life is not over. Count your blessings. Spend time with those you love. Choose to embrace life even though your loved one chose death.
- Anticipate that holidays, birthdays, and other special occasions will stir up painful memories. Plan a way to honor your loved one on these days. You might want to keep old traditions or incorporate new ones. Make sure that your own needs are met during these difficult times.

- Purpose to focus on how your loved one lived and not on the way he or she died. One choice on one day cannot cancel out the beauty of an entire life.

- If your grief remains overwhelming and interferes with your ability to function and relate to others, or if you have serious thoughts of harming yourself because of severe depression, please seek the help of a counselor, psychologist, pastor, or physician. Admitting the need for help is a step of courage, not a sign of weakness. The National Suicide Prevention Lifeline is 1-800-273-TALK (8255), www.suicidepreventionlifeline.org.

- In time, you might like to find a way to honor the life of your loved one. Make a scrapbook or plant a memorial flower garden. Start a scholarship fund or donate to a charity in his or her name.

- While your life has been forever changed, the pain will soften in time. The sun will shine again. Happiness will never mean you have stopped missing the person you lost. The return of joy is not a betrayal of love. Rather, it is a sign of healing and a necessary step in survival. Better days are coming.

For Immediate Help

National Suicide Prevention Lifeline
1-800-273-TALK (8255)
www.suicidepreventionlifeline.org

Suggested Resources

These sites provide clinical information on suicide, suggest tips for the survival or prevention of suicide, and can help in locating local support groups and Internet chat groups to connect with other survivors:

American Association of Suicidology (AAS)
5221 Wisconsin Avenue, NW
Washington, DC 20015
202-237-2280
www.suicidology.org
Provides information on suicide education and prevention as well as helpful resources for survivors.

American Foundation for Suicide Prevention (AFSP)
120 Wall Street
New York, NY 10005
888-333-AFSP (2377)
www.afsp.org
Excellent resource for continued survivor support as well as information on local conferences, support groups, and awareness walks. Extensive facts and statistics on suicide and information concerning prevention programs.

Suicide Survivors
www.suicidesurvivors.org
Provides support for suicide survivors.

Compassionate Friends

www.compassionatefriends.org

Offers support for those who are experiencing the death of a child.

Suicide Awareness Voices of Education (SAVE)

8120 Penn Ave. S., Suite 470

Bloomington, MN 55431

952-946-7998

www.save.org

Mental Health America

www.mentalhealthamerica.net

Survivors of Suicide

www.survivorsofsuicide.com

Provides support for suicide survivors.

Christian Online Support for Suicide Survivors

Survivors Road 2 Healing

www.road2healing.com

Provides support for suicide survivors.

Suggested Books from a Christian Perspective

Alcorn, Randy. *Heaven*. Carol Stream, IL: Tyndale, 2004.

Biebel, David B., and Suzanne L. Foster, MA. *Finding Your Way after the Suicide of Someone You Love*. Grand Rapids, MI: Zondervan, 2005.

Borntrager, Barbara. *A Mother Held Hostage: My Journey with Jon.* Springfield, MO: 21st Century Press, 2003.

Byers, Dale A. *Suicide: How God Sustained a Family.* Schaumburg, IL: Regular Baptist Press, 1991.

Cox, David, and Candy Arrington. *Aftershock: Help, Hope and Healing in the Wake of Suicide.* Nashville: Broadman & Holman Publishing Group, 2003.

Hsu, Albert. *Grieving a Suicide.* Downers Grove, IL: InterVarsity Press, 2002.

Sackette, Joyce. *Goodbye Jeanine: A Mother's Faith Journey after Her Daughter's Suicide.* Colorado Springs: NavPress, 2005.

Helpful Books from a Secular Perspective

Andersen, Jan. *Chasing Death: Losing a Child to Suicide.* Cambridge, UK: Perfect Publishers Ltd., 2009.

Bolton, Iris. *My Son, My Son.* Atlanta: Bolton Press, 1983.

Fine, Carla. *No Time to Say Good-bye: Surviving the Suicide of a Loved One.* New York: Doubleday, 1997.

Hoskins, Carol. *Surviving Your Child's Suicide: A Mother's Story.* N.p.: Protea Publishing Company, 2000.

Myers, Michael, and Carla Fine. *Touched by Suicide: Hope and Healing after Loss.* New York: Penguin Group, 2006.

Smolin, Ann, and John Guinan. *Healing after the Suicide of a Loved One.* New York: Fireside, an imprint of Simon & Schuster, 1993.

Underwood, Sandra. *Eric's Story: Surviving a Son's Suicide.* Bloomington, IN: Xlibris, 2004.

NOTES

Chapter 12

1. "Facts and Figures," American Foundation for Suicide Prevention, accessed September 11, 2014, www.afsp.org/understanding-suicide/facts-and-figures.

2. Candy Arrington, "Dispelling the Myths about Suicide," Christian Broadcasting Network, www.cbn.com/spirituallife/BibleStudyAndTheology/Perspectives/Arrington_Suicide_Myths.aspx.

3. John Samson, "How Alcohol and Drug Affect Depression," Articlesbase, August 5, 2008, www.articlesbase.com/mental-health-articles/how-alcohol-and-drug-affect-depression-510764.html.

4. "Suicide Prevention: Youth Suicide," Centers for Disease Control and Prevention, January 9, 2014, www.cdc.gov/violenceprevention/pub/youth_suicide.html.

5. Frank Newport, "In U.S., 77% Identify as Christian," Gallup Politics, December 24, 2012, www.gallup.com/poll/159548/identify-christian.aspx.

CPSIA information can be obtained at www.ICGtesting.com
Printed in the USA
BVOW07s0223280515

402014BV00002B/81/P